THE MAKING OF

# Master and Commander: The Far Side of the World

# THE MAKING OF

## *Master and Commander: The Far Side of the World*

## TOM McGREGOR

HarperCollins*Entertainment*
*An Imprint of* HarperCollins*Publishers*

HarperCollins*Entertainment*
An Imprint of HarperCollins*Publishers*
77–85 Fulham Palace Road,
Hammersmith, London W6 8JB

www.harpercollins.co.uk

Published by HarperCollins*Entertainment* 2003
1 3 5 7 9 8 6 4 2

A catalogue record for this book
is available from the British Library

ISBN 0 00 715771 1
ISBN 0 00 716398 3

Set in Granjon

Printed and bound at the Bath Press, Bath

PICTURE CREDITS

# CONTENTS

The author would like to thank the *Master and Commander: The Far Side of the World* production for their assistance with this book. Particular thanks to Gordon Laco, Mike Meehan, Martin Bibbings, and also to Virginia King, Monica Chakraverty, Terence Caven, Jo O'Neill, Bob Richard and David Vaughan-Thomas.

Twentieth Century Fox would like to thank Todd Arnow, Kimberley Cooper, Cathy Cultra, Alan B. Curtiss, Sam Goldwyn, Jr., Duncan Henderson, Edouard Henriques, Sandy O'Neill, Hutch Parker, Tom Rothman, Stephen Vaughan, Peter Weir and Andy Weltman.

# FOREWORD

On a rainy night over twelve years ago, I read my first Patrick O'Brian volume. I had found the book in my father-in-law's study in Old Lyme, Connecticut, ironically 'hard by' the then berth for the replica Royal Navy frigate, the HMS *Rose* which Fox eventually bought to help portray the HMS *Surprise*. As Jack and Stephen doggedly pursued the *Acheron* all the way to the far side of the world, my colleagues and I have chased the phantom of a movie version of O'Brian's unrivalled creation ever since. Sam Goldwyn, Jr., for whom I was fortunate enough to work at the time and who possesses a matchless eye for material, optioned the novels and communicated frequently with O'Brian until the author's death. Eventually Sam brought the project to Twentieth Century Fox, where Hutch Parker, President of Production for TCF, and another O'Brian devotee, toiled with Sam for years on the adaptation. Peter Chernin, President of News Corporation, Jim Gianopulos, Chairman of FFE, and many, many others at all levels of the company put hard work, thought, time, hope and, most essentially for any enterprise of such great economic risk, *faith*, into the film's creation. As is often the case with such undertakings, from the perspective of hindsight, it is impossible for us now to imagine any filmmaker other than Peter Weir, or any actor other than Russell Crowe, who could in the end have brought the *Surprise* and Lucky Jack Aubrey to such vibrant, yet faithful, life.

Indeed, it was Peter Weir who had the felicitous idea to begin the movie at sea, rather than on land as the first volume does, and found that the basic narrative outline of the tenth book, *The Far Side of the World*, was the most conducive to the structure of a motion picture. By starting right in with Jack and Stephen on the *Surprise* in action, we are thrown headlong into the heart, soul and essence of their world, a world never before rendered with the spectacle, scope and reality that modern filmmaking techniques can now recreate. Yet what the filmmakers have captured goes beyond the Naval experience; it is the essence of indelible characters. They are what make the novels unique and the film special. And what, we hope, will make it enduring.

In modern filmmaking, the voyage metaphor is a common one, but rarely so apt as here. *Master and Commander: The Far Side of the World*'s trip to the screen was long, arduous, dangerous and hard fought. It was also joyous, exhilarating and breathtaking (I, for one, will never forget the first incongruous sight, driving over the hills to our Fox Studios in Baja, of a towering British naval vessel rising, full sails to the wind, in the Mexican desert). The decade-plus that it took to journey from novels to cinemas worldwide was full of the familiar movie-business skirmishes between art and commerce, much as Jack and Stephen battle back and forth between action and reason. Yet, like the happy end of many of their travails, we believe the result will prove worth the effort; a film true in spirit to O'Brian which would have made the master proud had he lived to see it. It certainly makes all of us at Twentieth Century Fox proud.

Tom Rothman
Co-Chairman, Twentieth Century Fox

CHAPTER ONE

# Setting Sail

TREATMENT AND
DEVELOPMENT

Homer, Jane Austen and Butch Cassidy and the Sundance Kid are not the most likely of bedfellows. Yet, both together and separately, these were names commonly cited by people involved in adapting the novels of Patrick O'Brian to the big screen. Homer because he is credited with establishing the tradition of the epic sea voyage as a backdrop to the exploration of the human condition. Jane Austen because Patrick O'Brian has been endlessly compared to her; he wrote of her contemporary era and also celebrated the universal by means of the particular with wit, lightness of touch and an extraordinary depth of humanity. And Butch Cassidy and the Sundance Kid because it's arguably the greatest buddy movie of all time and because – again arguably – the most appealing element of O'Brian's Aubrey/Maturin books is the relationship between the two main protagonists.

Broadly, all three combine an epic canvas with very intense personal emotion. And that, again broadly, is a summation of this movie. Whether or not Patrick O'Brian would agree is a matter of conjecture (sadly, he died in 2000), but he did say that personalities, not principles or politics or even warfare, were of paramount importance in his novels. 'The essence of my novels is human relationships and how people treat each other. That seems to me to be what novels are for. They permit some pretty close examination of the human condition.'

Yet, as tools for that exploration, O'Brian wove lengthy, intricate and accurate tapestries around myriad aspects of the early nineteenth century. His concerns were not limited to seamanship and heroics in the Great Wars against France but extended to politics, language, recreation, diet, science and even furniture – as well as the lives of just about everyone he mentioned. Throughout this collection of twenty books, regarded as one of the greatest chronicles written in the last century, his stewards, gunners, carpenters and bosuns are almost as conspicuous as the characters of Jack Aubrey and Stephen Maturin.

Over a decade ago, Tom Rothman, now Co-Chairman of Twentieth Century Fox, then a Production Executive for Sam Goldwyn, Jr., had never heard of Patrick O'Brian – until he went on a vacation in rural Connecticut, which, perhaps fittingly, was plagued by 'British' weather. 'It rained incessantly,' he recalls, 'and I

PREVIOUS SPREAD *The* Surprise *in full sail, at sea. Patrick O'Brian described her as 'a trim, beautiful little eight and twenty... fast when she was well-handled.'*

OPPOSITE *'I scrape a little, sir. I torment a fiddle from time to time,' says Aubrey at his second meeting with Maturin.*

*'A man,' wrote Patrick O'Brian, 'who liked old ways and old wine, one of the comparatively few officers of his seniority who wore his hair long, clubbed at the back of his neck …'*

*'I loved the series,' says Peter Weir, 'but I really didn't think* Master & Commander *would make a very good movie. I said if I were going to do O'Brian, I'd start somewhere in the middle …'*

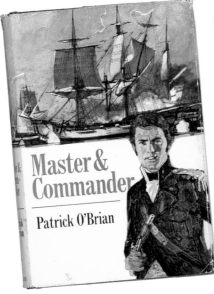

was prowling around the house looking for something to read. My father-in-law handed me a tattered copy of *Master & Commander* and said that if I could get through the first hundred pages or so I would probably like it. I did: I was hooked, lined and sinkered.'

So much so that he read the rest of the Aubrey/Maturin series (this was long before they'd reached cult bestseller status in the US) with a view to optioning them for film. It was, he admits, an unlikely and unwieldy subject for many reasons, not least because of the historical and literary nature of the subject matter.

'But,' he adds, 'I thought if it could be done right it would be wonderful for as many reasons. It could be one of the great buddy films of all time on a vastly romantic, thrilling canvas – a return to what great studio filmmaking used to be. Not a typical Hollywood "slam, bang, empty noise" movie but one of great substance, emotionality and texture. Analogous, maybe, to a David Lean movie.' He pauses. 'Look at *Lawrence of Arabia*: it was a character study – but it had some of the greatest action you'll ever see.'

Rothman then proposed the subject to Sam Goldwyn, who read the books, loved them, and subsequently met the author. By this time, O'Brian was well on the way to becoming a best-selling author, albeit one with a curiously ambivalent attitude towards fame and recognition. He also appeared to publicly affect a polite distaste as regards Hollywood. Sam Goldwyn is something of a

Hollywood renaissance figure, having produced or released projects ranging from *Sex, Lies and Videotape* and *Eat Drink Man Woman* to *Much Ado about Nothing* and *The Madness of King George*. Indeed, he was also the force behind a critically acclaimed documentary *The Mystery of Picasso* – relevant here because O'Brian wrote a much-lauded biography of Picasso. Meeting O'Brian and spending the best part of a week together can't have been a complete collision of cultures (especially given the fact they lunched together at the home of a mutual friend called Charlton Heston), yet it did reveal O'Brian's almost total ignorance of the world of film. As Sam Goldwyn recalls with a chuckle, 'I gave him a copy of *Much Ado* and *The Madness of King George* but I'm sure he didn't watch them. He said he never went to the cinema and that his TV didn't work…

'We talked a lot about how the *Hornblower* and *Sharpe* period of English history had always been very commercial. He told me that he thought that was because of the plots – and that what was missing from those was the lifestyle. Lifestyle was the essence of his books. He really wasn't interested in plot. He said it himself. He said he was far more interested in fabric. But,' continues Goldwyn, 'what his books do have are all these incidents. The plotting is what it is, but all of them have these *wonderful* incidents.'

Years down the line, those incidents and the fabric around them were exactly what Peter Weir concentrated on. In fact he went further, enriching that fabric with as much depth and texture as possible to evoke the spirit of O'Brian. As Tom

The Far Side of the World, *the tenth book, is in the exact middle of the series. 'Meticulously researched and heart-stoppingly vivid,' stated the* Washington Post. *'Few books boast the richly imagined central figures of these tales, or place them in such deeply researched settings.'*

*'I didn't like the idea of going up the rigging at first,' recalls Russell Crowe. 'But Jack does. So up the rigging you go …'*

Rothman says, 'the key is to be faithful to that *spirit* – and I will tell you categorically and absolutely that, because of my own sense of loyalty and obligation to Patrick O'Brian and the devotion of Peter Weir, Russell Crowe and the people at Fox, this film is one hundred per cent faithful.'

But Peter Weir initially turned down the project in the 1990s. 'I'm a great admirer of *Gallipoli*, *Witness* and *Picnic at Hanging Rock*,' says Sam Goldwyn, 'and I wanted to do something with Peter Weir. We'd been talking for a couple of years… I sent the O'Brian books to him and he took the trouble to read them but said he didn't want to do them.'

So the idea went through various stages of treatment, development and drafts without Peter Weir at the helm and, says Goldwyn, 'We very quickly ran into the problem of plot. We had a script which was more of an action picture and less of the pure fabric. Another problem was that we spent a lot of our time doing a very literal adaptation of the first book, painting in all the character background.'

Another major consideration – and putative problem – was that the books are set on land almost as much as on sea. 'It always interested me that the books always contrasted land with sea,' muses Goldwyn. 'I did go down that line with one draft, but it became too much of a buddy picture.'

Going on land also begs exploration of the inherent dichotomy of Jack: he is a complete master at sea yet inept on land. 'That always *did* interest me,' says Sam Goldwyn. 'He's a really complicated guy...'

Taking a film to dry land raises problems with the character of Stephen as well, particularly with regard to his mysterious espionage activities, yet as Peter Weir points out these activities had perhaps least relevance to the plot of *The Far Side of the World*. It's also worth mentioning that if they *were* addressed in a film, they would necessitate a corresponding sub-plot. And that would lead to all sorts of trouble.

As would women. Like restricting the film to the sea, keeping women out of the movie was something of a gamble. There are women a-plenty in the books. Yet, when O'Brian portrayed women on board (as he does in *The Far Side of the World*), it invariably signalled something toxic or calamitous. You can't, realistically, have a woman on board as a toxic calamity without descending into some sort of gruesome farce. And, as Sam Goldwyn put it, 'if there had been a

*'We live,' says Russell Crowe, 'on a planet of a hundred and thirty-eight foot by thirty foot.' Showing just how claustrophobic life on that planet could be is one of the aims of this movie.*

*Paul Bettany as Stephen Maturin (left) with Russell Crowe. 'The essence of my novels,' wrote Patrick O'Brian, 'is human relationships and how people treat each other... they permit some pretty close examination of the human condition.'*

*Unusually – for Hollywood, and indeed as an interpretation of O'Brian – there are no women in this movie. Yet when O'Brian portrayed women on board it invariably signalled something toxic or calamitous…*

*Peter Weir. 'I joined Patrick O'Brian's crew many voyages ago and travelled through his pages until volume twenty and his passing… I can do little but attempt to equal on film the power of his words.'*

woman on board in the film she'd have to be "the girl"…' And that would lead to a different film altogether, with things veering off in an Ava Gardner sort of direction. Tempting, perhaps, but also highly distracting.

These and other conundrums beset the project for years, and script drafts were further complicated by the fact that, ultimately, there are twenty books in the Aubrey/Maturin canon – and two hours in a film. 'You can,' says Tom Rothman, with reference to that welter of source material, 'either choose to do everything and you would do it poorly – or you could choose to do a few aspects very well.'

But until Peter Weir changed his mind, nobody could distil the material into those few aspects and treat them well. A couple of years after his meeting with Sam Goldwyn, the director was coming in to see Tom Rothman – now at Twentieth Century Fox – and Rothman wasn't going to let this one go. 'I really had to work up my nerve,' he says in a rather endearing, un-mogul-like fashion. 'There was a certain theatricality to the meeting: I'd had props make up what I imagined Jack's sword would look like and I had it behind my chair during the meeting…'

'He said,' recalls Peter Weir, 'that he wasn't going to pitch me a story, but that he was going to give me a gift. I thought that was a rather good approach… Then, to my genuine surprise, he gave me the sword. I took it and said, "O'Brian?" He said yes, he wanted me to take command. So I asked him,' he recalls with a grin, 'if I could keep the sword even if I didn't do the film. Because I wasn't going to do it. I said I couldn't do it – and I'd already said "no" to it. I read all the books,' he continues, 'I loved the series, but I really didn't think *Master & Commander* would make a very good movie. I said if I were going to do O'Brian, I'd start somewhere in the middle with one of the long voyages, and get to know these men when they were already friends. Tom told me to go away and do just that…'

'Peter,' says Rothman, 'cracked the problem; solved the riddle of how to film this. He said it was essentially a sea story and that the movie needed to start at sea; to have a very linear adventure with all the characterisation already there rather than harked back to. So his approach was to adapt the tenth book, *The Far Side of The World*. The exact middle.'

There are people who have already fired broadsides at the production for the

*Peter Weir flanked by Russell Crowe and Paul Bettany. 'With Aubrey and Maturin,' wrote Charlton Heston (a devotee of the books), 'the reader comes to understand and cherish their friendship perhaps as much as they do themselves.'*

*The nine-metre high and eleven-metre long model of the* Acheron. *Like her* Surprise *counterpart (seen behind her) she was built – and filmed – in New Zealand.*

loose interpretation of the word 'adapt' – particularly with reference to the nationality of the enemy ship. O'Brian's book is set in 1812, the year that America declared war against the British and allied itself with France in the Napoleonic Wars. Correspondingly, the enemy vessel is American – the *Norfolk*. In the film, the date is pre-Trafalgar 1805, and the vessel is the French *Acheron*. All sorts of theories have been propounded as to why the change was made. The most popular interpretation is that America cannot be seen to be the enemy.

'That's simply not true,' says a vehement Tom Rothman. 'It's nothing to do with that. Anyway, we're always making films with the Americans as bad guys…' The real reason is more prosaic than jingoistic – and has everything to do with the confines of the format. 'Even we [Americans] know about Napoleon,' continues Rothman. 'But it's so hard to explain to the uninitiated, in film, that the Americans became allies of the French.' To illustrate the point, he proposes a filmic explanation that would involve two or more characters sitting down and having a conversation about how the Americans have joined the war and are

*Another view of the* Acheron *model. The life-size ship had practically no rigging: scenes of her in full-sail are of this or of the computer generated version.*

now allies of Napoleon. It's long, convoluted (one would have to know *why* they had entered the war) and completely contradictory to the precept 'show, don't tell'.

Nor, vitally, would it add anything to the story. Particularly *this* story because, as Rothman says, 'the enemy isn't really personified here. In that regard this film is really unusual. Typically there would be a villainous captain who does something evil but, no, here it's a phantom ship. What you have are the broad strokes of good and evil.

'Who knows what will happen – the gods of the box office will tell us. But I do believe that in Peter Weir and Russell Crowe we have the only admiral and the only captain who could wage this war today. I can't think of another actor who could be "Lucky" Jack Aubrey and I don't know another film maker who could have pulled this off so true to O'Brian's spirit.'

*Land ahoy? No – and deliberately so. 'To re-evoke this genre,' says Peter Weir (pictured) 'I wanted to be at sea, to open the picture at sea and to hardly touch the land.'*

## Peter Weir's Adaptation

'It was the fabric, the clothes, the very nails on the deck... it was that I thought I had to acknowledge,' says Peter Weir. 'O'Brian is magnificent – a writer of the first order, and his greatness lies in his prose and in his characters; in bringing to life a world and an era on board a ship. But as for the plot, as for which ship they fought, where they were going... when I opened a book, I didn't really care whether they went to India or Australia or stayed in the Mediterranean.

'I really thought long and hard about it for about three months after he [Tom Rothman] gave me that sword,' continues the director. 'And I got to the point where not only did I want to start in the middle, but I wanted to trim off from the novel itself any of the shore scenes because, to re-evoke this genre, I wanted it to be as pure as possible. I didn't want any architecture. I didn't want crinolines, or carriages rolling down streets. I wanted to be at sea, to open the picture at sea and to hardly touch land.'

To that end, Peter Weir had to change the plot, as he freely admits, 'quite considerably'. As regards the on-shore/off-shore nature of the novel and, consequently, Jack's on-land persona and love affair with the Admiral's wife, he makes

*'I didn't want any architecture,' says Peter Weir. 'I didn't want crinolines, or carriages rolling down streets…' Instead he wanted to depict, as accurately as possible, every minute aspect of life at sea.*

a particularly interesting observation. 'By the time you'd shrunk that plot down, it would lend itself to parody. It's very hard, you know, to get into this genre without making a comedy: there *is* a certain tongue-in-cheek aspect to it all.' If he'd gone on land, he continues, he would have had to take care that O'Brian didn't tip into 'a kind of swashbuckling story'.

It's a fair point: O'Brian readers have long rejoiced in the author's crackling wit and his gentle poking of fun at Jack when, literally a fish out of water, he steps ashore. Over the course of twenty books and something like two million words, O'Brian had ample time to counterpoint these scenes against Jack's mastery of his sea-world – as well as to explore umpteen characters, a global tumult and an age shuddering with technological, scientific and theological transformations. The makers of this film had a couple of hours.

And this *is* a major Hollywood movie. The phrase may be hackneyed but the reality isn't. It cost a great deal of money and can't be made with *only* the O'Brian fan in mind, although there are bountiful fruits for the die-hard fan here. The movie has to have the broadest possible appeal within the confines of the material, and worldwide accessibility in its overall storyline.

*'O'Brian says he's a creature who's half-marine,' says Peter Weir of Jack Aubrey. 'He's meant to be at sea. He was born to it. He's a fish in water, if you like.'*

# AUBREY AND MATURIN

*'Aubrey-Maturin may yet rank with Athos-d'Artagnan or Holmes-Watson as part of the permanent literature of adventure'*

THE TIMES

With Jack Aubrey and Stephen Maturin, O'Brian created one of the most refined, quixotic and memorable literary double-acts in fiction. And one of the most unlikely pairings. Throughout the twenty novels that comprise the series, O'Brian repeatedly addresses the central axis and seeming dichotomy of their relationship; that '…he [Stephen] and Jack Aubrey were almost as unlike as men could be, unlike in nationality, religion, education, size, shape, profession, habit of mind…' This extract, from *The Ionian Mission*, concludes on the one note that unifies them: a love of music. Elucidating on that subject, O'Brian writes in *The Commodore* that 'Stephen once more contemplated on the apparent contradiction between the big, cheerful, florid sea-officer whom most people liked on sight but who would never have been described as subtle or capable of subtlety by any one of them (except perhaps his surviving opponents in battle) and the intricate, reflexive music he was now creating.'

There are clues a-plenty from these and countless other extracts (collated from the entire canon by Peter Weir as part of his research) about the relationship between the two men. 'I can do little,' says Weir, 'but attempt to equal on film the power of Patrick O'Brian's words.' In the broadest possible terms, the brooding ship's surgeon supplies the narration; the convivial ship's captain provides the action. It's a fusion of opposites. If Stephen is the candle that reflects the currents of air in a room, then Jack is the spark that lights the candle.

O'Brian was at his most compelling in delineating the relationship between Aubrey and Maturin. The latter's protean qualities provide the ideal counterpoint to Jack's more fixed yet flamboyant nature. Peter Weir has referred to Stephen as a product of the Enlightenment; a modern man in contrast to Jack who 'represents the type of man who's gone from the world, a warrior, almost a kind of samurai'. Again, that's the exposition at its broadest: beneath the waterline, in the nuances and gestures in the script, the full complexity of their relationship is revealed. Jack may be at the forefront – but Stephen is no sidekick. At one point in the film, Jack snaps at Stephen: 'Seeing the world through your smaller lenses is your prerogative'. Yet it is through the smaller lens of his microscope that Stephen quietly and unwittingly provides the answer – disguise – of how to tackle the *Acheron*. And it is Jack, with characteristic verve, who implements that disguise.

Peter Weir distilled the plot down to its essence. 'We have,' Weir says, 'a little ship and we have a big ship, and within that very simple story, I thought I could be as detailed and as rich as I like; adding some unpredictability to a very predictable storyline. I've tried to do everything I can in offering the possibility that you will experience life on board a British frigate with the hundred and ninety-seven men, boys, sheep and goats. And you'll take a long voyage from the coast of Brazil, round the Horn and up to the Galapagos Islands.'

So there you have it. But how did they do it?

## Reaching the Far Side of the World

'The secret of making good movies at sea,' says Producer Duncan Henderson, 'is to *not* go to sea.' And the secret of arriving at such a robust and seemingly bizarre conclusion is to know whereof you speak. Henderson, producer of the first *Harry Potter* film, executive produced *The Perfect Storm* and *Deep Blue Sea*. He also, along with every other Production Executive and Head of Department involved in this movie, watched innumerable films based wholly or partly at sea. These ranged from early Errol Flynn movies, to the 1984 *Bounty* (all of which was shot, incidentally, at sea), to movies that have all benefited from the entire weight of modern technology and Computer Generated Images (CGIs). The idea was to establish what worked at what period, what would work in 2003 and what wouldn't. There is a tape made by the production of clips from some fifty films studied, and they're not just sea stories: period films and films with land as well as sea battles all formed part of the research.

For this movie, even at treatment rather than script stage, it quickly became evident that whilst the story was almost exclusively at sea, filming it all at sea simply wasn't an option. 'You have to stay off the sea as much as possible. It's a drain financially,' says Henderson. 'And it's terribly slow because you're dictated to by the vagaries of the weather; by the sun and the sea and then by the wind to take a certain tack. I'd done *The Perfect Storm* and the trick there was to go out to water as little as possible. You do,' he adds, '*need* certain shots filmed at sea, but by the same token there are also things you *cannot* do at sea. You can't shoot a big storm scene if you're "in the doldrums" – and vice versa. You can't have a big sea battle. You can't, really, control the situation.'

'If you're making a film at sea,' says Peter Weir, 'you have to read all the books about making films at sea and learn from them. The instinct of a filmmaker is to go to sea, and you have to resist it, if you can,' he continues – rather ruefully, 'because all those books and the people who worked on those films tell you to. They tell you

that the sea is an unstable platform, that anything can happen and that it's very difficult. You have to get out there, get back, people are sick… and so on.'

Co-producer Todd Arnow picks up the theme and places it on the bottom line. 'The more you can control, the more bang you can get for your buck. Yes, it's important that you do have footage out at sea – that's really how you sell it – but there are multiple reasons why you can't shoot at sea all the time.' He reiterates the need for storms and battles and also, bearing in

mind that this was a five-month shoot, the requirements and indeed sanity of the people involved. 'Your cast and crew would not be able to withstand being out at sea under normal conditions, let alone under filming conditions. You're trying to get performances but you can't perform normally – you're out at sea.'

Filming at sea on a square-rigged vessel for any period of time is actually a nightmare, even without engaging in battle or being blasted by storms. The set moves up and down and from side to side in a manner that you can't control; there are too many people on board (some of whom are seasick) and the sun and sails can create havoc with lighting. And going out to sea and back again adds hours to a daily schedule. There are other, less immediately obvious problems as well: life on the ocean wave can be incredibly claustrophobic, you're stuck on a small ship for twelve hours a day – and if you get wet in your heavy woollen

*Life imitating art – with the help of CGIs. The raft lowered from the* Surprise *and set adrift to act as a decoy for the* Acheron. *Filmed using the 'real' ship and life-size raft in the tank (below), CGI shots (above) add swell of the sea and grade the colour of the sky.*

# EXCAVATING THE WOODEN WORLD

*'It's a kind of archaeology – and it's thrilling'*

## PETER WEIR

'You have to try not to be a bore about this,' says Peter Weir of the monumental amount of research behind this film. He jokes that he could 'nail you to the floor' by telling you all about it. The opposite, in fact, is true: it's very difficult to be bored by passion. 'You get so interested,' he continues, 'so into this world from your reading and visits to museums and underwater dives and travels on the *Endeavour*. Forget making a movie; you just get into the fabric of the extraordinary shipboard life of the era.'

So little was known about the reality of that life, and in particular life below decks (not much was even known to the general public at the time) that everything had to be painstakingly researched. 'Here's a crazy detail, right?' offers the director. 'Espadrilles. Those canvas shoes with rope soles that you can buy anywhere in the world. I was sure they must come from the navy so I began to check. We got back

as far as we could and finally got in touch with a shop in Spain which has been making them for a couple of hundred years: they said, yes, originally we made those for the Spanish Navy...' Weir pauses and then grins at the thought of another detail he researched. 'Toilet paper. I won't go into that. But, boy, did I go into that – a search for what they used as toilet paper...'

Arcane and lavatorial minutiae apart, Weir also trawled through – with evident relish – publications that both pre- and post-dated Nelson's era. He rattles off references to Tobias Smollett, Samuel Pepys, Frederick Marryat and Herman Melville and, back in the present day, admits

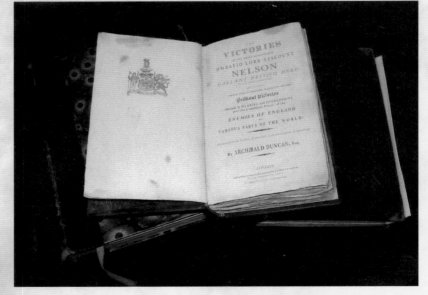

*A tiny detail in the film, but crafted with as much care as the the ships themselves: the book about Nelson given by Jack to the convalescent Blakeney.*

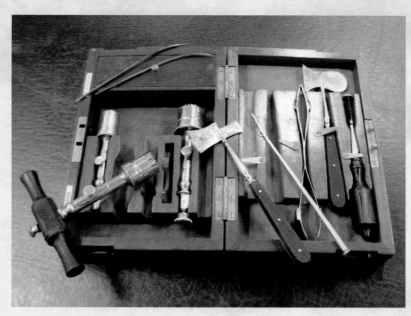

rather sheepishly that when Production Designer Bill Sandell left before filming began he couldn't replace him because 'well… what would they do? I realized I knew more than I could ever ask someone to do. They'd have to read all the books and sail on the *Endeavour* and do the museums and so on…'

And whilst Peter Weir spearheaded every aspect of the years of research into every detail, he's the first to admit he wasn't always right. 'When we were in London doing our research at Greenwich, the "holy of holies" of British naval history [one of the first ports of call for both the director and his wife Wendy, the Costume Designer on this film], I remember I bought a hat. I thought I'd done a terrific job. It was a British sea captain's hat of the period and I took it to Wendy and her team to show it off. They said "It's French,"' he recalls. 'I said how on earth can you tell? They pointed to the beading that runs down the side. Then I asked if it was from the period and they said no, it was slightly out…'

So the hat went out too. Inaccuracy is anathema here. Peter Weir even researched sounds of tall ships of the period and acquired a book on early eighteenth-century spectacles (for Stephen Maturin) but, again, 'I don't want to bore anyone – and for God's sake, you've got to enjoy the acting and the drama, the high adventure. Yet I do hope the detail will make a difference to watching the film; that it's as close as you can get to the impossible idea of travelling back to the past.' He comments with a laugh that if you brought an eighteenth-century seaman back from the dead, 'he'd probably say: "I'll give you six out of ten"…'

Who knows – but hopefully Weir would be awarded ten out of ten for trying. Take, for example, the lanterns on the *Surprise*: they're exact copies from those on Nelson's *Victory*. 'When I was visiting, they said they liked my approach to detail so they gave me one: not an original – a copy of an original. They gave me permission to take it off the property. I remember this incredible tingling feeling walking out of the gates of the dockyard carrying a lantern from the *Victory* to bring to Mexico in my luggage, to have copied and put on our ship…'

*Filming the storm scene in the tank at Baja. No CGI in this shot: the storm may not have been real (it was blazing hot weather) but the wind and water hurled at the actors was authentic enough.*

*The model of the* Surprise *being filmed in New Zealand for part of the storm scene. Intercut with frames of the full-size ship in Mexico as well as Computer Generated Images, the edited version plays as one seamless scene.*

officer's uniform then you stay wet. You also have to learn to walk with slightly splayed feet and, in the early days, many people have to deal with the 'hangover' of being at sea: falling over in the shower back at base is the most common after-effect. 'Plain sailing' it is not.

'Ultimately,' continues Arnow, 'we determined that it would be in our best interest to have two ships; one that we could go out to sea in, and one that we could put in a controlled environment.' A controlled environment in this context is, by definition, an open-air tank with an ocean view. Unless you're filming exclusively with model

ships, that is the only option and, within that option, there are three alternative locations: Melbourne, Malta and Mexico. The tank at the latter, near the US border in Baja California, was built specifically for filming *Titanic*, and is the newest and the most sophisticated. And that's where, in January 2002, roughly three years after Tom Rothman presented Peter Weir with Jack Aubrey's sword, the production finally landed. Filming started four months later – not because of any unforeseen delay but because the vital ingredient still had to be added: the ship.

'At the end of the day,' says Duncan Henderson, 'there is basically the ship, the ship and the ship.' A ship, to reiterate Peter Weir's words, that would take a long voyage from the coast of Brazil, round the Horn and up to the Galapagos Islands.

Except that it doesn't. Apart from the Galapagos landing – which was actually filmed, uniquely for a movie, on the Galapagos Islands – the production didn't go anywhere during principal photography. All filming was done in Baja and on the ship.

*Land only features when the* Surprise *reaches the Galapagos Islands. Here on its black volcanic rock are Lord Blakeney (Max Pirkis), Padeen (John de Santis) and Stephen Maturin (Paul Bettany).*

Or rather, the ships. The *Acheron* aside, there are two ships, and both of them play the *Surprise*. Given the criteria established during the lengthy period of research and script development, this isn't in itself unexpected. As mentioned, it was imperative that some filming had to be at sea – hence one ship – whilst the majority had to be done in the controlled environment of a tank. You cannot transfer a full-size ocean-going square-rigged ship from the sea to a tank.

*The model of the* Surprise, *seen from a human scale. This really was built – and filmed – on the far side of the world: New Zealand.*

And when you look at the script and what they do to the ship, the need for a the tank environment becomes more apparent. 'You're destroying different parts of it or disguising it at different times,' says Duncan Henderson. 'We keep changing the look of the ship, so we needed flexibility. We needed to have construction people working on it at the same time as we were filming.' In short, they needed the tank at Baja and its attendant studio and facilities. A relief, no doubt, to Todd Arnow. On a 'normal' day, he had seven hundred people to look after on this production… Baja became not a studio but a small city.

OPPOSITE *Even the shipwrights who built the* Surprise *in her various incarnations have difficulty telling them apart. This is the 'tank' ship.*

## *Patrick O'Brian's* Surprise

Patrick O'Brian's *Surprise* was 'a trim, beautiful little eight and twenty, French built with a bluff bow and lovely lines, weatherly, stiff, a fine sea boat, fast when she was well-handled, roomy, dry'. (Patrick O'Brian, HMS *Surprise*).

Prior to captaining her, Jack Aubrey served on her as a midshipman. He 'had spent hours and hours banished to the masthead – had done most of his reading there – had carved his initials on the cap: were they still to be seen? She was old, to be sure, and called for nursing; but what a ship to command.'

And she was no invention either, but based on a real frigate of the same name that had begun its life as the French *Unité*, built in Le Havre in 1794 and, in 1796, captured by the British, renamed and commandeered into their own

*Another view of the full-size, tank-bound version of the* Surprise.

navy. At several junctures throughout the Aubrey/Maturin series, however, Jack mentions that the *Surprise* is older than HMS *Irresistible*, launched in 1787. For this reference, O'Brian 'borrowed' another French ship called, confusingly, *Unity* [or sometimes *Unité*] in its English incarnation – a ship that was indeed built slightly before *Irresistible*. Even the Royal Navy confused the two ships in various service listings – a confusion not helped by the fact that both ships were sold by the Admiralty in 1802. The received opinion in O'Brian circles is that the fictional *Surprise* was an amalgam of both ships – and possibly several more.

But from the point of view of the production, the real *Surprise* was the key to the ship they would use. Although she sailed on in fiction through thirteen Aubrey/Maturin novels, she disappeared from history – presumed broken-up – in 1802. But, crucially, her plans survive. Drawn by dockyard shipwrights after her capture, they are to be found in the National Maritime Museum at Greenwich in London.

Copies were put into the hands of the film production team. So was a detailed description of the ship by eminent historian N.A.M. Rodger. All they had to do now was find a ship that looked like her – or that they could convert into her. And then make a duplicate for the tank.

You're dealing in a limited market when it comes to scouring the world for tall ships that are both accurate replicas of eighteenth-century originals and available to people who look like they might fire cannonballs at them. The replica of Captain Cook's *Endeavour* (properly, HM *Bark Endeavour*) is one of the few three-masted square riggers of the correct era and, although not a frigate, is widely regarded as accurate in all respects. But she's based in Australia, owned by a charitable trust – and not for sale or hire.

But – and it's an important but – the *Endeavour* played a significant role in the genesis of this project. As part of his research, Peter Weir took two journeys on the ship (Duncan Henderson, Director of Photography Russell Boyd and Executive Producer Alan Curtiss accompanied him on his second, four-day voyage). 'It's the most *beautiful* recreation of Cook's vessel,' says Weir. 'And it's the only replica vessel afloat that has a period-accurate lower deck. You go on as sail-training crew and you live as they did. You sleep in hammocks and work watches and go up the rigging and do all of that. It was a unique opportunity to experience the life… you get into this strange cycle. It's just work, sleep, eat… work, sleep, eat. And you're working in a team. It gave me an invaluable insight into how it must have been in those days.' Alan Curtiss, who worked on the project practically from inception, adds 'The *Endeavour* experience was our boot camp training: it was very, very valuable.' Particularly from his point of view: Curtiss broke down the script (a monumental task), scheduling what would be filmed where and in what sequence. 'It would, for example,' he says, after his *Endeavour* trip, 'have been lunacy to shoot a storm sequence at sea.'

*Peter Weir discussing a set-up (he doesn't do formal rehearsals). Note how crowded the ship is with its full complement of cast and crew. It may be a controlled environment, but it's also a cramped one.*

Of his own trip, Duncan Henderson says that 'our four-day taste gave us some idea of what we could and could not do. We climbed the ropes, went up to the tops and set sails and did safety things and so on.' These first-hand experiences reaped rewards when it came to filming. 'We were told we'd need stunt guys for climbing the rigging and that sort of thing. We were able to say "no, we've done it so actors and extras can do it as well".' Henderson pauses and grins. 'Well, only if they felt comfortable doing it. Some people didn't like the idea, or they were afraid of heights so they didn't have to.' That statement also provides a clue to the nature of filming this project. The actors in this film didn't rehearse scenes (Peter Weir doesn't, anyway, do formal rehearsals). Instead, they learned – and this *was* compulsory – all about life on board a ship, to the extent that they were so familiar with the ship, rigging, weaponry and drills that they could live their roles, not just act them. More of which later.

The *Endeavour* subsequently played a more direct role in this film. In March 2002, she sailed around Cape Horn. The voyage itself was pre-arranged and nothing to do with this production but – vitally – they were able to place two camera crews (film and video) on board. The voyage round the Cape being an integral part – both thematically and visually – of the movie, the hope was to get footage that, eight months later, could be edited digitally, via computer, into the film shot on location. Helen Elswit, Visual Effects Producer, says they were more fortunate than they expected. 'We were hoping the *Endeavour* would be in a storm – which it was. We were hoping for snow – which we got. There's footage of an iceberg, and even of an albatross.' 'And we're going to use it,' says Peter Weir. 'Isn't that a great story?'

So when in the movie you see the Cape from the point of view of the *Surprise* at sea, it isn't an approximation of the Cape. It *is* the Cape. And whilst only a tiny portion of this footage will be graded and edited into the final film, getting it in the first place was quite a coup. Very few tall ships – indeed very few ships – sail round Cape Horn nowadays. The Panama Canal precludes the necessity to sail to where two oceans converge to form the most ferocious stretch of water in the world. It brings the far side of the world rather closer. Which is where, in terms of finding a ship, this production was heading.

# *The* Rose

The search for a ship to play the *Surprise* took Peter Weir and production executives all over the world, and finally ended in Newport, Rhode Island, with the tall ship the *Rose*. Coincidentally, Patrick O'Brian had visited the ship in 1995 and was recorded politely expressing approval of its gammoning rope! Care, and indeed love, had been lavished on her by owners Kaye and Jan Williams, but she needed a little work…

Built in Nova Scotia in 1970 and modelled – not to the highest degree of accuracy – on a ship of the same name constructed in Hull, England, in 1757, the

*Used for years as a sail-training ship, the* Rose *underwent a substantial overhaul – including complete re-rigging – to become the* Surprise.

*Rose* served for years as a sail-training vessel. She wasn't in the best shape when the production bought her. Nor, more to the point, did she look particularly like O'Brian's *Surprise*.

Nick Truelove, a shipwright with *Endeavour* experience who saw the *Rose* in Rhode Island, said 'we were quite amused when we saw her. I think I said I'd like to get a chainsaw and hack the back off her: the ship wasn't what it was supposed to be. There were head rails on her and

*On the voyage to refit the* Rose, *the crew encountered weather like this and the ship was badly damaged. A very good resaon for filming storms in a safe environment (this shot was filmed in the tank) and adding CGIs.*

many other things which were wrong as regards historical accuracy. It wasn't built as an authentic frigate anyway – and Peter was after a frigate because that's what the book was based on.'

But Peter Weir got his frigate – several months later. That's one of the reasons why the production bought the ship rather than renting her (it helped, of course, that she was for sale). You can't, realistically, rent a ship and do what this production did to it with any hope of handing her back in her original state. The substantial alterations took place in San Diego, close to the studio in Baja. But first the *Rose* needed to get there. Andy Reay-Ellers, who worked on the ship several times over a period of years and went on to become an integral part of the production, helped sail her there.

'The Captain needed three mates for the two-month journey from Newport, and through the Panama Canal, to San Diego. At that point someone on the film said they might want me afterwards because they were going to build another part of the *Rose* on a big tank of water or something.'

Reay-Ellers laughs at that memory. 'I didn't envisage what they meant… Not at all.' What they in fact wanted was for him to help build a full-scale, exact replica of the refitted *Rose* in the tank at Baja. Nor did he envisage his subsequent incarnation as Sailing Master of the refurbished *Rose* and Technical Advisor on the film. But that's what happens – and it happened to a lot of people in this story – when you have unrivalled expertise in the world of tall ships.

'Rule number one about leaving Rhode Island in a ship like this on a non-stop journey to California is not to do it in the first week of January,' explains Reay-Ellers. 'So that's what we did. We had to, to meet the refit schedule.'

It turned out to be a pretty dramatic journey. Within a few days they encountered huge storms. 'We had winds of over seventy knots. Things on board that ship which had been rock solid and in place since she had been built just broke loose. Puerto Rico was our first stop after leaving Rhode Island, so we did repairs there and then headed for Panama. But what we didn't know was that there was other damage within the core of the rig…' What followed was something of a precursor to what the production had to deal with when filming the script – and shows why they had to film it in a controlled environment.

'We were sailing along in glorious Caribbean weather,' says Reay-Ellers, 'and, in the space of about ten seconds, the topgallant mast just blew to pieces. I was on deck and for some reason I glanced up and watched it go. I can still see it quite vividly, right now. It took the topgallant sail on its yard, and that fell forward, landing on some rigging. We're talking about stuff that's a hundred, a hundred and ten feet, off the deck. That lot landed on lines which go to the next sail, so broke *that* yard… we went from sailing beautifully to having all these spars and riggings just dangling like some mobile from hell…'

And, to make matters worse, night was falling. They had to do immediate repairs at sea, sailing by necessity off the wind and in the dark. In the morning they discovered the crack in the main topmast, and the fact that the huge main topsail, hanging on the piece of mast above the break, could not be struck (lowered, in layman's terms).

This unplanned drama, featuring a very expensive ship and some valuable people, illustrates why making a movie set at sea is more practical if you avoid, as much as possible, risky things like actually sailing out to sea. Yet, as Reay-Ellers points out, he wished they'd had some movie cameras on board. 'We could have got some pretty exciting footage.' Some very expensive footage and, possibly, some deceased actors.

Leon Poindexter, who had worked as a shipwright on the *Rose* for several years – and who has built square-riggers listed in the National Register of Historic Places – went on, like Nick Truelove and Andy Reay-Ellers, to become one of Peter Weir's invaluable on-set advisors. Although not on the voyage to San Diego (he was in Los Angeles working with the Art Department), he remarks that, whilst Andy Reay-Ellers had the 'luxury' of reaching a port in which to complete repairs, it was – as shown in the film – commonplace to do major repairs at sea. 'They had a skilled carpenter and his mates and, of course, the rest of the crew to help out. And they carried a lot of extra materials on board.' Tony Dolan, the actor who went on to play ship's carpenter Mr Lamb, points out that 'we have a mizzen mast that gets snapped in the first engagement. I have to repair that. We also have to deal with Cape Horn, which is notorious for its bad weather, and where we sustain even more damage. And, of course, we lose our mizzen mast completely. And then we have to repair again for the final engagement…'

A cycle of damage and repair that simply couldn't be filmed at sea. The *Rose*, in fact, wasn't going to be damaged at all. But, once at San Diego, she was going to transmogrify into the *Surprise*. No easy task in the first place: especially compounded by the fact that San Diego, in Leon Poindexter's words, 'isn't a place where you can just go and cut lumber in the forest like we're used to doing.' San Diego is situated between the desert and the deep blue sea. Materials had to be shipped in as well as a construction crew – at times as many as fifty – to refit the ship to represent, in every possible detail, Patrick O'Brian's *Surprise*.

The acclaimed novelist A.S. Byatt said of Patrick O'Brian that 'He has a passionate desire to tell you everything; from what kind of wood something was made of down to what knife and fork people ate with.' It's a quote that could apply to Peter Weir: he researched every detail of all aspects of this film. And the mention of cutlery is remarkably apposite: in this film there's a fleeting glimpse of an exact copy of the combination knife and fork that Nelson ate with. It really is a case of 'blink and you miss it' – but it's there, part of the fabric.

It is, however, the detail of the ship that will attract the most audience attention and, in this respect, the director had invaluable input from Leon Poindexter and other shipwrights and historians. The basic construction of the decking and timbering had to be French, but, because the *Surprise* had been owned by the British for many years, many details had to be correspondingly English. 'Often a movie is ruined because the details aren't right,' comments Poindexter. 'The historical accuracy just isn't there and there are so many flaws that it just becomes kind of silly. Also, Patrick O'Brian was very fussy about detail and getting it right, and I think we've also gone to great lengths. We had access to the Admiralty deck plans,' he continues. 'And that gave us the deck height, the number of chain pumps, the location of the Brodie stove and all those details that we would otherwise be guessing at. I think Patrick O'Brian fans will be looking for those things, and I think they'll find them here.' Then, with a smile, he adds that 'I actually think they'll be quite amused by the lengths we've gone to: including things like the cable lifters in the mooring cables. One of the things we found out was that, in the southern hemisphere, the mooring cable was fastened to the anchor on the starboard side. It's just one of those details, but it was there – and that's why we included it.'

Major changes, however, involved removing some of the superstructure (which was too modern), changing the hull and the bulwarks and, after two months, a move from dry dock in San Diego to Ensenada in Baja (close to the studio) where she would be based during filming. The majority of filming, however, was done on the 'twin' ship which, at the same time as the *Rose* was being refitted, was under construction at the studio in Baja. 'Once we had determined what to do with the *Rose*,' says Todd Arnow, 'We obviously had to build the *Surprise* – and they had to be a dead match.' To the untrained eye, they do indeed look identical…

Here the rigging was completely rebuilt, and ten sails were added to make the requisite total of twenty-seven – and a total of more than twenty-five miles of rope. The rope, in fact, provides a good illustration of just how far the production went to

*The early stages of ship construction, in the studio compound at Baja.*

replicate the rigging of an original vessel of the time. No steel wire here: all the rope was specially woven and wrapped in an outer layer to make it look like the tarred hemp of the period. Even minute details were observed. Chief rigger Jim Barry points out that 'it was quite well known that they used left-hand lay for quite a few of the bigger ropes. It was quite visible. So we have ropes with both left-hand and right-hand lay.' The weight of all those miles of rope, incidentally, is five tons.

At the same time as the carpenters and riggers were working on this ship, set dressers from the art department were swarming all over her. 'I'm still amazed,' says Andy Reay-Ellers, 'at how they would come and paint something bright and beautiful and then come back the next day and start ageing it, putting layer upon layer of paint to get something that doesn't look brand new. The ship is brand new in construction terms – just a few months old. But it's been made to look twenty or thirty years old, with parts of it all chewed up and aged, and with twenty thousand miles under its belt.'

Leon Poindexter, who worked closely with the art department, says they had to be extremely careful with the weathering. 'We found a lot of documentation as to how much paint was supplied to these ships. One captain actually wrote back to the Admiralty Board asking that, with the amount of paint they'd given him, did they want him to paint the starboard side or the larboard? They worked hard to keep their ships clean, but they didn't really have the paint – and the sea is a very difficult environment in which to maintain a ship.'

And, as mentioned, it's a difficult environment in which to make a movie. Which is why the *Rose*, in her new incarnation as the *Surprise*, was used for less than fifteen days (out of a total of ninety-four) of principal photography. The rest of those days had very little to do with life on the ocean wave…

# SYNOPSIS OF THE STORY

'HMS *Surprise*, 28 guns. 197 souls. Coast of Brazil, April 1805' reads the caption as the movie begins. A lantern-bearer illuminates the largely sleeping ship, but Captain Jack Aubrey, in the Great Cabin, is reading his instructions. We catch a glimpse: '…intercept French Privateer *Acheron*. You will sink, burn or take her as a prize…'

At dawn the next day, a towering, dark shape is sighted, bearing down on the *Surprise* and opening fire as she emerges from the fog. Jack and his first Lieutenant, Pullings, quickly establish that the ship has eighteen-pound cannons – twice the size of their own. Jack needs to get closer to inflict damage. Despite carnage, a direct hit to the gun-deck and further damage, Jack orders fire as the two ships pass broadside to broadside.

Most of the *Surprise*'s cannonfire ricochets off the other ship. The *Surprise*'s wheel is shattered, a swinging boom catches seaman Joe Plaice on the skull, Midshipman Blakeney's right arm is severely injured and Jack's forehead is scored by flying debris. Pullings has already been knocked unconscious. Then the coxswain Bonden informs Jack that the rudder has been shot away below the waterline. They are, as seaman Slade mourns, 'fish in a barrel' ripe for boarding by the crew of the other vessel – now identifiable from her lettering as the *Acheron*. Jack orders the men to lower the boats and tow the *Surprise* to the sanctuary of the fog bank. They disappear into a whiteout.

That night the tally is revealed: nine dead and seventeen wounded. Jack wonders how, after seven weeks looking for the *Acheron*, she found

them instead. Ship's doctor Stephen Maturin, mentions that, like the English and every other nationality, the French have their spies… Jack informs the crew that they will repair at sea rather than heading for Jamaica or home. It's a huge undertaking, but Jack is adamant they will follow the *Acheron* to the south seas.

During and after repairs, we see life on board the *Surprise* – at its best and worst. Stephen operates on the wounded, amputating Blakeney's arm and trepanning Joe Plaice's skull. Jack and Stephen accompany each other (rather well) on the violin and cello. Lieutenant Mowett is revealed to be a poet. A keen amateur natural scientist, Stephen examines sea-creatures as gun-practice happens below – and, as they approach Brazil where they will find a mail-ship, letters are written to loved ones at home.

Anchoring off a bay in Brazil, they learn that the *Acheron* called here before them – and will be three weeks ahead of them. Blakeney evinces an interest in Stephen's natural history, and in particular of phasmidae – creatures that disguise themselves in order to survive.

Later, at sea and at dawn, Blakeney bursts into Jack's cabin: the *Acheron* has been sighted in the distance and is heading towards them. Jack calculates that they're speedy enough to evade her until nightfall – by which time they have built a raft which, lowered into the water under the 'command' of Midshipman Calamy, and bearing lanterns to mimic the stern of the *Surprise*, is later cut adrift. The ruse works and they evade the ship that is now regarded amongst the superstitious crew as something of a phantom. Jack now reverses roles and starts chasing her – to Cape Horn if necessary. Most of the crew applaud the move: if they capture the ship she becomes their prize.

They reach the Cape but fail to capture the *Acheron*: the French ship disappears and the *Surprise* is damaged in a ferocious storm. The mizzen mast snaps and crashes into the sea. Warley, a topman, falls with it and drowns as the rigging has to be cut loose to save the ship. Midshipman Hollom is blamed: already unpopular for being weak, he is now seen as a Jonah – a harbinger of bad luck – by the seamen.

From the heat of Brazil through the storms of the Cape, through icebergs of the Antarctic – and a diet of penguin – to the doldrums. The ship is becalmed, water is low, and a reluctant Jack is obliged to have a seaman, Nagle, flogged for insubordination to Hollom. Later, haunting noises from the sea terrify the crew – according to Joe Plaice, it's the Jonah signalling to the phantom ship. Taunted beyond endurance, Hollom commits suicide in front of Blakeney, his only friend.

Jack has already revealed to Stephen, that his orders were to follow the French ship only as far as the Cape. But he's determined to follow the *Acheron* to where he's 'sure as there are carts to horses' she'll be heading: the Galapagos Islands. For the ship, a privateer, is on a mission (as revealed in the parts of Jack's instructions we didn't see), to attack the British whaling fleet and commandeer valuable whale oil.

The crew reaches the islands. Hogg, a whaling captain, confirms Jack's suspicions. The *Acheron* has taken his oil as booty and his crew as prisoners – and she's not far ahead of them. Jack orders the *Surprise* to sail after her, thereby breaking his promise to Stephen that he can roam the fabled habitat of unusual species to his heart's content.

Just off the islands, Captain Howard of the Marines attempts to shoot a huge sea bird, misses, and shoots Stephen in the stomach instead. The swell is too great to operate so Jack abandons his pursuit and turns back to the Galapagos. Stephen is carried to dry land and operates on himself, with Higgins and a queasy Jack in attendance. A recuperating Stephen is out collecting specimens with Blakeney and his servant Padeen when he spots the *Acheron* in the distance. The trio retreat to the *Surprise* where Jack, taking his cue from the natural world, decides to disguise his ship, phasmid-like, as a whaler in order to lure the *Acheron* towards them. The tactic works, and as the *Acheron* approaches they run out the guns and the colours and enter into battle. This time, surprise is on their side…

*Russell Crowe as Jack Aubrey. 'He has a natural authority,' says Peter Weir. 'He was born to be a captain: a captain of actors and a captain of a ship.'*

# CHAPTER TWO

## The Far Side of the World

### FILMING IN BAJA, MEXICO

ost people don't stop here. They head south, to watch the fabled Grey
Whales of Baja; or north to San Diego. Here, on the humdrum Highway 1,
there's a clutch of shops selling tawdry tourist artefacts and, on the opposite side, a
bunch of warehouses. It's all pretty prosaic – and a stunningly improbable setting
for some of the greatest sea voyages in both fact and fiction.

Drive through the gates towards the warehouses and you become convinced
that you're in the midst of a large manufacturing plant. Which indeed you are…
Fox Studios in Baja is a vast, 40-acre complex built for, and dedicated to, manufacturing illusions. *Titanic* sailed from here: she also met her iceberg here. And,
for six months, all of *Master and Commander: The Far Side of the World* was here.

The greatest illusion of the complex is that the centrepiece, the huge open-air
water tank, merges seamlessly with the Pacific Ocean. It doesn't. But, gazing out
to sea, it's impossible to tell where the 17-million-gallon tank ends and the sea
begins – until a bicycle appears on the horizon. Watching the cyclist pedal across
the ocean is a highly peculiar sensation. Or perhaps sensationally peculiar; it takes
a moment or two to register that your mind isn't playing tricks, that there is actu-

PREVIOUS SPREAD,
OPPOSITE AND
BELOW *The* Surprise
*in the tank at Baja.
Nearly all of the
journey to the far
side of the world
was filmed here, in
the deep section of the
6-acre tank. The
aerial view gives lie
to the notion of the
infinite horizon seen
from ground level:
the tank does not run
into the ocean.*

ally a road (part of the studio) between
the tank and the Pacific and, beyond it, a
40-ft drop until you reach the ocean.

The aquatic cyclist appears possible
because the seaward side of the tank has
in fact been constructed like an infinity
swimming pool, with the water gently
flowing over the side – although the paraphernalia surrounding it is rather different
from the palm trees and deck chairs of
pool life. Here, instead, are the nuts and
bolts of the film-world: great barn-like
sound stages, construction workshops,
storage areas and physical plant facilities.

# THE TANK

There are actually four tanks at Fox Studios. The main, outdoor one is the dominant feature of the whole studio complex with a capacity of nearly 20 million gallons of seawater and a total area of over 360,000 square ft. Built in 1996 to house the 750-ft replica of the ship *Titanic*, it was altered the following year to meet requirements of the Bond film *Tomorrow Never Dies*. This is when the 'infinite' horizon (in reality a 450-ft long weir overflow on the seaward side) was added.

Most of the tank is 3.5 ft deep, although there are two deeper sections, one 100 ft by 200 ft which can be filled to a depth of 40 ft and the other 30 ft by 300 ft, which is 15 ft deep. The gimbal was built in the 40 ft deep section.

This is the only such tank in the world serviced by a 162-ft tower crane, which can be used as a lighting and camera platform as

well as for light construction. Spare a thought for the man who operates the crane: he climbs up in the morning and stays there all day, with supplies being hoisted to him in a high-tech bucket. A giant, 300-ton crawler crane was also used to lift both the *Surprise* (in three sections) onto the gimbal and the *Acheron* (in four sections) into the tank. The reason why the two ships were built in sections was because the crane, despite its enormity, couldn't lift them whole. The rope used on the *Surprise* alone weighs five tons.

Tank Two is inside an insulated sound stage (100 x 200 x 29 ft) and has a capacity of just over 7.3 million gallons – again of seawater. Uniquely, it has a 90 x 160 ft steel platform supported by a hydraulic system capable of lifting, lowering and tilting sets weighing up to 0.6 million pounds. For anyone who remembers the *Titanic* tilting towards its watery grave, it did so here. The *Master and Commander* production didn't fill this tank but used the stage for a below-decks set. (All filming of the interior of the ships was done on specially built sets on the sound stages.)

Tanks Three and Four are, by comparison, small (maximum half a million gallons) and can accommodate both fresh and sea water. Tank Three is outdoors and abuts the main tank whilst Tank Four is indoors.

*The drained main tank reveals its three different depths. The central section (where the gimbal was constructed and upon which the* Surprise *was placed) is 40 ft deep, abutted by a 15 ft deep trench. The surrounding area of the tank is 3.5 ft deep.*

## *HMS* Surprise

And here, too, is where the *Surprise*, in all weathers and navigating several seas, sailed across the far side of the world – without moving. That last bit isn't strictly true. The ship *does* move: it pitches up and down and it rolls from side to side. It can also turn round – a manoeuvre that takes all night because it is controlled, not by the wind and the waves and the weather but by another phenomenon: a gimbal.

To the naked eye – even the gimlet eye of expert shipwrights – the *Surprise*, as she sits in the water, is in every way a mirror-image of the *Rose*. But below the waterline it's a different story. The ship doesn't have a keel; she sits on her gimbal. Generally, gimbals consist of two or three pivoted rings at right angles to each other, providing free suspension for compasses and chronometers. They are not, generally, designed and built at the bottom of a tank in order to both support and direct the movements of a full-size ship.

But that's precisely what this gimbal was designed for. Months before filming began, the (drained) tank was a construction site instead of an ocean. Most of the

*The* Surprise *on the gimbal that dictates her movements. Construction of the ship (and the gimbal) now completed, the tank is being filled – a process that takes nearly 40 hours.*

*Too large to be hoisted by crane in one piece, the* Surprise *and* Acheron *were built in sections. Lowered onto the gimbal, they slotted seamlessly together, the joins invisible to the naked eye.*

*A 162-ft tower crane was used during filming by camera crews. It can traverse the entire length and breadth of the tank.*

tank is 3.5 ft deep, and it is here that the *Surprise* was built. A central section, however, is 40 ft deep and this is where the gimbal was constructed. There's something faintly Victorian-looking about the mammoth structure in its antediluvian state: hugely sophisticated, it also has a brutality about it that is reminiscent of the great age of steel. But this is the age of the tall ship, and the next stage of development was to put the *Surprise* on top of the gimbal, flood the tank, and create the ongoing illusion of a ship at sea.

Again, there is nothing Lilliputian about the *Surprise*: it's a full-size ship and can't be picked up and moved: even by a 300-ton crawler crane. That's why – again this is invisible even to the most sharp-eyed of shipwrights – the ship was constructed in three sections, each slotting together like some giant wooden toy. The crane lifted it, section by section, onto the gimbal.

Looking at the ship on the filled tank and against the infinite horizon, there's nothing to suggest that it is possible to separate her, vertically, into three sections. Nor is there any hint of the gimbal beneath. Other irregularities are also invisible: the fact that the ship is built of pine and not a hardwood like oak. (Pine is easier to work with, and it's also cheaper.) Basically, what one sees is a carbon-copy of the refitted *Rose*: everything that meets the eye is a perfectly-realised vision of Patrick O'Brian's *Surprise*. Yes, the production had a wealth of knowledge and advice from fleets of technical and historical experts, but the overall result is quite a feat considering that the man in charge of the project (gimbal as well as ship), Construction Co-ordinator Gary Deaton, is a set-builder, not a shipwright.

Chief Rigger Jim Barry was in charge of the rigging group, and had his hand – literally – on every mile of rope and every one of the six hundred blocks and iron hooks specially made for the *Surprise*. No commercially made hooks darken the deck of this ship. 'They're very square nowadays,' says Barry. 'These rounder ones give a more authentic look.' He should know as he has participated in the building of several tall ships – some for museums – although he's never been involved in a project for film. And he's remarkably sanguine about the startling difference between this and previous projects: the timescale. 'Normally you'd have about a year to build a boat like this. We had sixteen weeks from start to finish.' And they started, according to fellow rigger Jennifer Convey, from biggest to smallest; 'building shrouds to keep the masts up and prevent them from tacking fore and aft. From there you go to the building blocks, strapping them so that they'll stay in place; then lofting out the running rigging so that you'll have the proper length of rope you need...' There's a clue here to one of the challenges that faced the set designers: the arcane language used

*Every element of the* Surprise *was painstakingly researched to produce, on the tank at Baja, a perfectly realised vision of the ship described by Patrick O'Brian.*

*The ship rolling on the gimbal. The 'ocean' is only 3 ft deep.*

*The ship may be stranded in a tank, but everything about the rigging is fully functional. There are twenty-one sails and more than twenty-five miles of rope.*

by shipwrights. To build these ships, they had to be bilingual in 'gunwhales', 'beakheads', 'bulkheads' and 'taffrail'.

Timescale (and language) apart, the particular differences of this project were gimbal-orientated. 'I didn't know how hard this boat would be used,' comments Jim Barry. 'It surprised me that it was used far more than the *Rose*. All the parts of the rigging are moving all the time… ropes loosen as they get worn, so it needs a lot of maintenance. But the big difference is that a normal ship would be out to sea and the whole thing would be driven by the wind. Here the stresses are concentrated on one part of the ship.'

The point, here, is that the ship is firmly attached to the gimbal and, with wind created by jet engines (think giant hair-dryers) aimed at specific parts of the ship during, for example, the storm scene, there is a potential pressure problem. Add to that the dump-tanks that send hundreds of gallons of water pouring down chutes onto the ship, and the problems of being marooned on a gimbal become more apparent.

They are especially clear to Sailing Master Andy Reay-Ellers, who says that the construction people actually erred on the side of caution. 'I hope I'm not giving

# THE MONKEY BAR

Crouching amidst the barn-like constructions at Baja is an idiosyncratic little building, designed by Ingrid Weir, and quirkily christened the Monkey Bar. It's made of corrugated iron – a bit like an old-fashioned aeroplane hangar – yet some of its furnishings come from the first-class lounge of the *Titanic*. The Monkey Bar has nothing much to do with the film: its firmly behind the scenes. Yet its existence provides an interesting insight into the psychology of this movie.

There are twenty-five principal actors here – twenty-three of them from the UK – and from the outset it was decided that, even if they weren't required for filming for fairly lengthy periods, they would be here for the entire five-month shoot. That's unusual. It's also potentially extremely boring. Being on a film set for months on end can be a pretty dreary and often isolating experience. Furthermore, having actors hanging around in hotel rooms or dressing rooms doesn't exactly echo the spirit of an ensemble piece – especially one set on a ship in 1805.

'There's no place to meet,' says Peter Weir. 'So I began to think a club – a gentleman's club in England – how could we do that? And it somehow evolved into the Monkey Bar.'

The idea was deliberate; the name accidental. It derived from the point in the script where the *Surprise* lands on the coast of Brazil. Stephen Maturin's servant Padeen draws a picture of one of the monkeys they see and, rather than do this drawing themselves, the art department asked every other department to have a go themselves – partly because it was decided that Padeen's drawing would be slightly crude and certainly unprofessional. The winning entry was chosen to feature in the film, the others were hung here, giving the room its name.

But this is more than just a private club for the principal actors. Producer Duncan Henderson calls it a 'colonial outpost for the Brits' and, in many ways, it's exactly that. It's deliberately retro: there's no TV here and no music. There is, admittedly, a tiny alcove with a computer for sending and receiving e-mails, but the rest of the place is given over to activities – pool, chess and other board games – that require actors to interact with each other. Beyond anything else, it invites conversation – and if you don't want to talk, there's always the collection of Patrick O'Brian novels to read.

There is also a spectacularly annoying parrot but, its raucous shrieks apart, the Monkey Bar has proved to be an amazing morale booster for the actors. It seems so obvious that you wonder why it's not the norm for a film like this – but it isn't. And it's unheard of for a director to look genuinely horrified at the idea of marching into somewhere on his own set as if he owned the place. As Peter Weir points out he, like nearly everyone else, was denied membership on the grounds of not having a speaking role in this film. He was, however, allowed in as a guest. As long as he behaved.

anything away here, but the gimbal can only heel over to a certain degree, and there are certain scenes when the ship is supposed to be even further over. So people on deck accentuate grappling to keep on their feet, and the camera is tipped at an angle to add to the motion. So I'm thinking this isn't as bad as it should be in the conditions we're supposed to be experiencing, but then I realise that we are seeing it, we are feeling it – and the camera is adding to it.' Equally importantly, the camera can detract from the gimballing. The technocrane used by the camera crew has a libra head that can work on three axes and can counter-act the ship's movement. If the camera constantly rolled and pitched with the ship then so, in the cinema, would the audience. A line has to be drawn between authenticity and throwing up in a multiplex.

So to the camera. It is very easy to forget that whilst cameras don't lie, they do play fast and loose with the truth. What you see on-screen is only part of the bigger picture off-screen. The storm scene, for example, is all *real* – but it is an amalgam of different realities. There are the frames used from the deck of the *Endeavour*; footage from the decks of both the *Surprise* and the *Rose* and, additionally, there are Computer Generated Images (CGIs). The result is a seamless sequence bearing no trace of the disparate elements, filmed at different locations, weeks or months apart.

From the comfort and warmth of the production office, Producer Duncan Henderson provides a robust explanation of why, out on the tank, he is heaping indignities in the shape of several tons of water, flung at dizzying speeds, on his actors. 'You can't shoot a storm sequence at sea, but you can set it up so that it looks as dangerous as being at sea. You can,' he adds enthusiastically, 'pour so

*Preparing for the storm scene. The dump tanks (right) send hundreds of gallons of water down chutes. The jet engines and the propellor fans suspended on the crane (left) create a high-speed maelstrom.*

'We had eleven days of storm sequence,' says Russell Crowe (centre left). 'At one point we had the jet engines as close as four metres from the cast...'

much water on them that you can sweep them right across the deck. You can have jet engines blowing it at them at 100 miles per hour.' It sounds truly grim. 'Oh yes,' finishes Henderson, 'they really are experiencing a storm. But you can be sure that no one will die.'

Henderson's last point is really rather serious: it's pretty nasty out there on the tank. And quite surreal: the water may only be 3.5 ft deep but the *Surprise* is lurching about on its gimbal, four enormous dump-tanks are hurling vast volumes of water down a chute onto the deck and wind machines are battering the ship and all aboard her. Bryan Dick (Nagle) is in the thick of it and, as he later recalls, 'There are these industrial-sized fans, water cannons, jet machines, you're dripping wet, covered in water and you're standing at a 45-degree angle with an axe in your hand. It's as it would have been. It's quite scary.'

This is how they filmed rounding the cauldron of Cape Horn in a ferocious storm with the additional horror of going the 'wrong way' – straight into the westerlies. Historically, most ships avoided doing so, but here Jack is chasing the *Acheron* or, as Joe Plaice puts it, 'the devilship is leading us into a trap.' And someone *does* die: Warley. Joe Morgan, who plays the character, is on the top yard of the mizzen mast, desperately trying to rope in the sails, and he needs help.

*The* Surprise *leaning drunkenly on its gimbal. This is the lull before the storm and, in filmic terms, before the addition of CGIs. With digitally graded sea and sky, this image will look more like a 3D version of the painting on page 51.*

'Hollom can't reach me,' Morgan explains, 'and suddenly the whole top end of the mast snaps off and falls into the sea. It's still attached to the ship by ropes. I'm thrown and I'm desperately trying to swim for the mast; they're throwing barrels to me and Nagle (my best friend) is shouting encouragement. Then the ship starts to broach because the wreckage of the mast is pulling her down. They need to cut it free. So unless they do so and destroy all my hopes of getting back to the ship, the whole ship is going to tip into the sea.' The whole thing is over in minutes, but Joe recalls a different reality: 'Two weeks drowning in the tank.'

Acting ain't all fun, then. Besides the water tanks and jet engines, the tank is crawling with little support and safety vessels, all the actors (and crew) are often stumbling around for real, and they're getting drenched on a daily basis. Yes, they're wearing wetsuits under their costumes but, for the uniformed officers in particular, those costumes are heavy in the first place – and leaden when wet. And, although there are safety wires attached to those who have to climb the rigging, they are being bombarded with as much weather as modern technology can muster.

Fast-forward to the editing suite and this scene is injected with a unique third dimension – real footage taken from the *Endeavour* going round the Cape. 'We got some sensational "plates", as we call them, to build in,' says Peter Weir. 'So the water we use within this part of the film will actually be the water from the Horn. I rather like that detail…'

*Life was never lonely on the ocean wave. The* Surprise *is constantly surrounded by supply vessels and equipment for the film crew.*

It has to be reiterated (revealing a slightly different reality) that the ship on the tank is indeed a perfectly realised vision of Patrick O'Brian's *Surprise* – as long as the eye doesn't venture to the top of the fore and main masts. They're too short. The reality of those missing sections comes later – with the CGIs.

Visual effects Producer Helen Elswit explains that, in calculating the combined weight of the ship, the equipment, cast and crew on the load-bearing gimbal, a compromise had to be reached. There was a danger of excess weight. So the compromise was not to complete the masts in question. 'It makes life considerably more interesting,' she remarks, 'because Peter Weir has to constantly frame down so as not to show them. Only on the widest shots will we have to put the topgallant masts in.' It's worth remembering that there were very few wide shots of the *Surprise* in the first place: nearly all the wide-angle shots of the *Surprise* at sea are actually shots of the *Rose*.

The best example, however, of a CGI is to be found on board the *Acheron*, the French ship that plays cat and mouse – and havoc – with the *Surprise* and the British whaling fleet…

*The storm sequence takes on another dimension with the addition of CGIs.*

# *The* Acheron

'Build her,' says Jack of the *Acheron* at one point. 'So that she sits in the palm of my hand.' Jack is addressing Warley, who saw the 'phantom' ship being built in Boston but who can't describe, in words, what is special about her.

Yes, she is special as a ship, but she's also highly significant as a metaphor. Her antecedents lurk in the Hades of Greek mythology: she is named after one of the infernal rivers of the underworld, the eponymous *Acheron*, meaning 'river of woe'. The name has sometimes been used synonymously with the whole of the lower world. So she's a metaphor for hell itself – and Joe Plaice isn't far off the mark when he refers to her as having 'the devil at the wheel'. The ship isn't just Jack's enemy: she's his obsession and his nemesis.

The river Acheron (or Ackeron) first appears in literature in Homer's *Odyssey* – twenty-four centuries before the era in which this story is set. The *Odyssey* tells of Ulysses' ten-year wanderings home to Ithaca after the defeat of the Trojans, and its title has long become synonymous with any long journey. Ever since the time of that epic, storytellers have found the community of a wooden ship and the rhythm of a voyage a natural stage against which to deploy human emotion. O'Brian was one of them. He makes countless references to the *Odyssey* (and the *Iliad*), while Jack and Stephen – and Mowett – are well versed in those tales from antiquity. Stephen's attitude to the *Odyssey* is particularly interesting – and typically vigorous. He recalls that 'a great many busy fellows… found out hidden meanings in Homer by the score…' True to form, he's pretty dismissive of these 'inky boobies' and their hidden meanings – and then launches into a muscular preference for the *Iliad* because it's 'as clear as the sun at midday that as well as being the great epic of the world, the *Iliad* is a continued outcry against adultery.'

The actual ship on which the *Acheron* was largely modelled, the USS *Constitution*, was Boston-built and is now berthed there as a museum piece: the oldest commissioned warship in the world that is still afloat. Launched in 1797 to defend the fledgling US nation, she was designed to be powerful enough to outfight any enemy warship the same size, yet fast enough to outsail a larger opponent.

*First Lieutenant Pullings (James D'Arcy) and The Master Allen (Robert Pugh) examine the model of the* Acheron *built by seaman Warley. The double hull is the secret of her strength.*

The *Acheron* also pays homage to its literary inspiration: Patrick O'Brian's fictional *Norfolk* which, in turn, was based on the USS *Essex*. The *Essex* was an exceptionally fast ship, which, in 1812, became the first US warship to venture into the South Pacific, with instructions to disrupt the hugely lucrative British whaling trade. Two years later, she was hunted down by two British ships and, after lengthy combat, almost destroyed.

One of the *Constitution*'s claims to fame, also in 1812, was a historic battle with HMS *Guerrière*. After an hour of manoeuvring and firing, the battle became a short-range slugfest, with the mizzenmast of the British ship quickly falling and going overboard. Further parallels with the *Acheron/Surprise* confrontation appear when, in the same battle, a British sailor allegedly saw a cannonball bounce off the *Constitution*'s side and exclaimed that 'Her sides are made of iron!' Thus was born the ship's nickname 'Old Ironsides'.

In December of that year, the *Constitution* was engaged in a lengthy battle off the coast of Brazil with HMS *Java* (this conflict is described and referred to on several occasions in O'Brian's Aubrey/Maturin canon). Again victorious, she all but destroyed the British ship, consolidating her position as one of the Royal Navy's most formidable opponents. The *Acheron* therefore wove its way into the script through an intricate web of fact and fiction – mirroring O'Brian's *Norfolk*.

A vivid and impressive history for a ship that was built in the back lot at Baja. But look at the work in progress – and the result – and you're watching something quite as magisterial as the other ships. Digital scanning of the *Constitution*

*The* Acheron *under construction in the back lot at Baja.*

# THE FINAL BATTLE

'I had no idea,' says Jack to Stephen, 'a study of nature could advance the art of naval warfare'. He's referring to Stephen's discovery on the Galapagos of a 'phasmid', the stick insect that disguises itself to hide from its predators. It's a discovery that leads directly to the final confrontation between the *Surprise* and the predatory *Acheron*, with the former ship disguised as a whaler.

This confrontation is loosely referred to on set as 'the final battle scene', which is something of a misnomer because, from initial contact to boarding and to the capture of the French vessel, the action actually races through approximately fifty scenes. In layman's terms, that baldly means one hell of a lot of planning.

It's the reason why the full-size *Acheron* was built in the first place. And it's why more than 150 extras have been drafted in, and why, from the point of Stunt Co-ordinator Doug Coleman, 'it's a three-month process to get it all organised. There are 400 people with weapons,' he explains, 'and they all have something to do. Crossing from ship to ship; dying, stabbing, fighting with everything from muskets to swords and cutlasses and from hand-to-hand.' And one of the problems as regards rehearsing this was that the *Acheron* was

still being built at the initial choreography stage: it wasn't beside the *Surprise* in the tank to practise crossing from ship to ship.

Another fundamental consideration for Doug Coleman is that a lot of people are injured or die here. Historical accuracy is one thing, but slaughtering actors is cruel and expensive. So safety is one of the highest priorities: a safety that underpins what Coleman calls the 'high-risk illusion' and 'choreographed chaos' behind what one actually sees. The riskier work involved stuntmen – fifty of them in total – playing fall guys, working as fight technicians and in the tank for underwater scenes. No stunt-doubles, however, were used for any of the action here, so all the actors and extras had to be trained to create the illusion of – and yet avoid – complete carnage. As one actor put it, 'you're thinking about how to fight in a tiny, tiny space.

*The final battle, with the crew of the* Surprise *boarding the beleaguered* Acheron.

*Each sequence in the final battle had to be minutely choreographed and rehearsed months before filming.*

You maybe had fifty men fighting each other in a few feet. The damage must have been horrific.'

Swordmaster Dan Speaker started training for this even before filming began. 'The targeting and distancing that you create during your training period has got to be a safe place to be, so you put a lot of energy into the swings. Yet at the same time you have to put as much energy into stopping them – without making it look like you're doing that. It's very difficult to do.' And furthermore, 'about the hardest thing to do when you're fighting is to block the blow that you as an actor know is coming in, but that you as a character does not. Making that work is a really difficult proposition.'

Probably the biggest fighting sequence was a twenty-four-man attack against Jack Aubrey as he goes into the lower deck of the *Acheron*. Speaker and his fellow Swordmaster – his wife Jan Bryant – started choreographing this as soon as they got to Baja. And a little secret here: there are women in this film. Jan Bryant features prominently as a French privateer. 'I get killed several times,' she laughs, 'I get killed by, I think, four of the principals, and most notably by Russell Crowe, on the gun deck of the *Acheron*.' It's probably safe to

say that no viewer will ever be able to tell which pirate was a woman. No disrespect to Bryant – rather a testament to the skills deployed in costume and make-up – but even in close-up she looks like a man. But she looks good as a woman too: you can see her on-screen as Catherine Zeta-Jones's stunt double in the sword-fighting scenes in *The Mask of Zorro*.

Even before weapons training began, storyboarding for this section of the film was well under way. Every angle of every scene has to be minutely pre-planned months in advance but, as Storyboard Artist Christopher Buchinski says 'with script changes and as you get closer to shooting time, you want to get as accurate as possible. With the choreography, stunts and CGIs, it's almost like drawing dance steps.'

Except that this isn't a dance – far from it. As Jack Aubrey puts it whilst rousing the crew to action 'England is under threat of invasion, and though we be on the far side of the world, this ship is our home. This ship is England… and a blow dealt to Napoleon's tyranny here will be felt just as keenly as one dealt on our own doorstep. So every hand to his rope or gun, quick's the word and sharp's the action. After all, surprise is on our side…'

meant that her hull and deck and any details shown on film were indeed exact replicas of that ship, but the *Acheron* is more complicated than that. We know that she's American-built, but we also know that her present incarnation is as a French privateer. She would almost certainly have been altered by the French, and the movie's Art Department catered for this in elements of her design (see Chapter Three), and experts will notice this. But as on-board expert Gordon Laco says, further complexities are hinted at. 'She's not a warship; she's a privateer, so why do you see glimpses of a Napoleonic "N" on her? Why would a privateer carry an Imperial symbol?' Nobody really knows, but (see Chapter Four), there are some intriguing theories and historical precedents.

In other respects, the *Acheron* is also less complicated than she appears. Whilst vastly impressive, she doesn't pretend to be complete. Her starboard side has frames but is unplanked (this will be CGI'd in) and her rigging, from inception, was basically as it is seen in the battle at the end of the film. Forlorn at best: wrecked at worst. So Jack's words to Warley – 'build her so that she sits in the palm of my hand' – were prescient ones indeed. When you see the ship from a distance and in full sail, you're seeing CGIs based on storyboards, which, in turn, are based on models.

The storyboards are a crucial ingredient of every film. The models (there are also miniatures of the *Surprise*) are vital for several reasons. One of them, says Christopher Buchinski, 'is continuity. And accuracy. Different things happen at different stages... bits of ships are blown away, especially when you get to the final battle scene. You have to nail everything down to the millimetre for the CGIs. You have to be incredibly precise. If you're just a little off, then you're way off.'

*The figurehead of the* Acheron, *a stylised dragon.*

Sometimes – for closer shots showing the deck – the CGI is composited together with shots of the 'real' ship. At other times, with the *Acheron*, you're seeing a virtual ship.

But how do you put the wind in her sails; how do you make virtual rigging act the same way as real rigging? There's nothing haphazard about the way these ships move: everything is dictated by the wind and a multitude of sails. So you need someone like Andy Reay-Ellers to draw a complete, working sail plan.

'One of the things I have to do is write out how they should set the sails. This is strange to me because, of course, no person will ever lay hands on ropes and canvas to do that: it's going to be the guys at computer keyboards – and their level of dedication is just the same as everyone else's. The accuracy they're working towards is amazing. When I've said that a certain sail would have to be set, the animation is there, but they're asking me things like exactly when the line would pull on the sail and where the stress would be on the sail. As a ship rocks, how much does the cloth stretch? Do you think that's a factor of ten per cent stretch… where exactly is the belly of the sail? It's mind-boggling, and to marry that together with the real shots is going to be just fascinating.'

But the 'real' *Acheron* is equally fascinating. And seeing her in the tank, beside the *Surprise*, is also quite mind-boggling. For a start, it's more than a little surreal seeing two full-size ships in a tank 3 ft deep and surrounded by the paraphernalia of a film set. The *Surprise* is utterly believable: the *Acheron*, above the height of about 30 ft, is in need of a helping hand from the CGIs. Instead of a full foremast, she sports a strange, helix-shaped object that looks clashingly anachronistic but that will, of course, never be seen on film. The twenty-first century intrusion is a tracking point for the visual effects, with different-coloured balls from which the digitising process can extrapolate the direction of the sails and the position of the fighting tops.

Desolation Island *by Geoff Hunt, whose paintings are specially commissioned for the covers of Patrick O'Brian's novels. Here, one ship follows another into stormy waters. Sounds familiar…*

Wind forward the story, as it were, to the final battle scene, when the two ships are together and 'joined' by the fallen mast (built as a prop) of the *Acheron*, and anything modern becomes irrelevant and is anyway out of sight. The crew of the *Surprise* are about to board the French ship, a scene that is filmed almost exclusively close-up and with several hand-held cameras. There are no computerised images here; no add-ons. And given that there are hundreds of people in this scene, everything had to be minutely prepared and choreographed. Looking at the intricate set-up just before the cameras start rolling, the set seems eerily reminiscent of a painting.

And that's exactly what it is. Peter Weir has a portfolio of paintings and illustrations which inspired much of this film, and there is one in particular, of one of Nelson's battles, that he used as a blueprint for this set. The angle of the two ships, with the mast in the sea between them, is identical. The mid-battle arrangement of the rigging is the same. The only missing element, for the moment, are the people, although there are a few shudderingly realistic dead bodies caught up in the fallen mast, which again echo the painting.

That painting, in common with other references gleaned during years of research, serves as a reminder of one of the fundamental goals of this film: to convey a depth, a texture and a history based on much more than cinematic alchemy alone.

Counterpoint the painting with a close examination of the deck of the *Surprise* itself – pre the battle set-up – and a three-dimensional representation of the fruits of those researches reveals itself. On the quarterdeck, Jack's personal nine-pound cannons are faithfully reproduced to match the ones O'Brian gave him in the novel – right down to the detachable aprons covering the vents.

Further forward is the double-wheel, again an accurate reproduction. The only concession to filmmaking is, as ever, an invisible one. Because only portions of the lower decks were constructed here, the rope tackles work on a pulley system. But the wheel still displays the characteristics of being connected to the tiller and rudder.

Beside the wheel, the binnacle is complete with all the correct navigational instruments of the time. Some of the drawers containing them are never opened in the film – but the instruments are there. Set designer Marco Nero recalls that designing the binnacle box was a challenge. 'It doesn't have any nails: it *can't* have any nails, because that affects the compass. So I designed it without nails. That was pretty difficult.' And this, remember, is on a ship that isn't actually going anywhere. The irony is that, like a compass, it sits on a gimbal.

Further forward on the weather deck, the waist of the vessel houses the three

*The only concession to filmmaking on the deck of the* Surprise *is an invisible one. The rope tackles work on a pulley system, which is attached to the ship's wheel.*

ships' boats which, when removed, show the open gratings. They, in turn, can be removed to reveal the midships section of the gun deck; in those days sometimes called the 'slaughterhouse'. There is a portion of the fully functional gun deck visible here – but only a portion. The rest of it is elsewhere.

But the camera never ventures below decks here. It shows glimpses: down the companionway leading to Jack's quarters or, as mentioned, through the open gratings to the midships' guns. The interior of the ship is elsewhere at Fox Baja; on other sets, each built to the same painstaking degree of accuracy as the ships themselves.

Above deck, the fighting tops have been crafted and prepared right down to details you'll never see on film. The ribbing on the top surface of the fighting tops is exactly as displayed in Admiralty diagrams of the time. And the Marines' ammunition boxes are there, invisible to the camera but primed all the same.

## Filming in the Galapagos

'It beats looking at hospitals,' grins Location Manager Mike Meehan, a man whose career has seen him scout everything from, well, hospitals, to one of the sparkling jewels of this film and indeed his career – the Galapagos Islands.

You can improvise and imitate many things in order to match a script, but when you have a unique environment of worldwide renown there is really no substitute; no stunt double that can play the Galapagos Islands. The only problem

*A map of the Galapagos Islands drawn by the officers of the* Beagle *in 1835.*

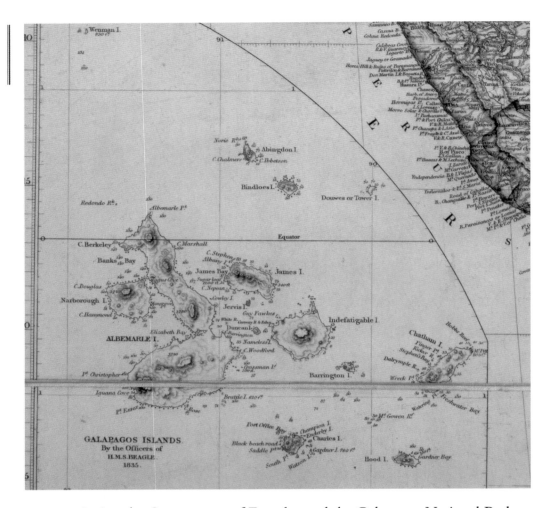

was convincing the Government of Ecuador and the Galapagos National Park to let them film here. 'There was a certain amount of trepidation on their part,' says Meehan (probably an understatement), 'so putting them at ease was the biggest challenge. They feared we wouldn't share their respect for the islands.'

It's worth pausing to reflect on just how respected these islands are. No one is allowed here on a whim: every visiting party has to come via a regulated tour operator and is only allowed to visit designated areas under the supervision of licensed guides. There are no hotels: you have to leave the islands at dusk and spend the night on your boat. It's forbidden to take food onto the islands, and anything you do bring has to be inspected and sterilised. 'You or me coming in just our sneakers with just one bag is one thing,' says Meehan, 'but if you bring anything bigger they're worried about bugs… about the simplest things. And God forbid we bring anything in.'

This isn't paranoia; it's preservation. The fauna of the Galapagos are unique: the co-existence and, vitally, variation of differing animals of the same species placed the islands firmly in the history – and mystery – books long before Charles Darwin visited in 1835. But it was Darwin's five-week visit that catapulted the

islands into global recognition: they led him to arrive at his theory of natural selection, still the most important theory in biology.

Given Stephen Maturin's consuming interest in biology in 1805 in this script, it's important to remember that Darwin, as he freely admitted, was not the first person to arrive at the theory of evolution itself. That theory (at the time called 'transformism') had been around since the end of the previous century. What was unknown – the mystery that Darwin addressed in *The Origin of Species* in 1859 – was how and why complex organisms developed gradually from simpler ones.

So Stephen Maturin knew all about the notions being bandied around with such excitement in natural history circles. And he knew how extraordinarily heretical they were: these theories flew straight in the face of creationism. His desperation to get to the islands, then, is understandable. 'At the time,' says Paul

*The Galapagos Islands, home to some very chilled-out fur sea lions and (below) to insects of great appeal to Maturin. 'For some unearthly reason,' says Paul Bettany, 'he has a complete fascination for insects. I don't. To be honest, I loathe them. They terrify me…'*

*Stephen Maturin (Paul Bettany), Lord Blakeney (Max Pirkis) and Padeen (John de Santis), off to collect samples on the Galapagos Islands.*

Bettany who plays the character, 'if you opened up a creature, people thought you were looking into the mind of God. And that's part of the dichotomy of Maturin: he's a staunch Catholic and yet he's a naturalist: he's involved in a pastime that will kill God.'

So the Galapagos Islands were pivotal to both the geography and the psychology of the film. And, as mentioned, nowhere else on earth can replicate those islands. 'You can CGI a lot of things,' says Mike Meehan, 'but when you have a marine iguana moving across the land or a frigate bird flying... the crazy, wonderful mystery of a blue-footed booby as it stares at you with those beady bird's eyes... that's not, truly, something you can generate in a computer. Having an actor interact with those wonderful animals in this incredible environment,' he concludes with passion, 'really isn't something you can do with two tennis balls on a stick.' (This is a reference to the technique that would otherwise have to be used: the tennis balls and stick would at least give the hapless thespian something to interact with, and would later be replaced, by computer, with animation.)

It's not difficult to spot that Mike Meehan has a profound respect for the islands and their occupants. A respect he conveyed to the authorities. After three recces (the first of which was over three years ago) and many meetings with the Ecuadorian Government and the Galapagos Natural Park, permission was granted to film on the Galapagos – the first ever non-documentary footage to be filmed there. It helped a great deal that there's nothing gratuitous or whimsical about the desire to film there: the script clearly delineated Maturin's motives for wanting to land there. And Jack's motive – the primary motive – is again firmly grounded in history. Since the 1790s the British whaling fleet had indeed been

*OPPOSITE Pinnacle Rock on the Galapagos Island of Barthelemy.*

ABOVE *Marine iguanas sporting unusual headgear. The crest that grows on their heads is, in fact, almost as hard as the black lava rock against which these reptiles can be almost indistinguishable.*

plundering the waters around the Galapagos Islands. That fleet was almost destroyed in 1813 by the *Acheron*'s linear antecedent – USS *Essex*, or O'Brian's *Norfolk*. The captain of that ship, incidentally, was responsible for releasing onto the island of Santiago the current scourge of the Galapagos: goats.

'We have been given an opportunity which no one else has been afforded,' says Mike Meehan of the unique privilege granted to them. 'I think we're honoured, lucky and, yes, extremely privileged. But we are working with the National Park: they set the parameters.'

And they're not in the business of granting concessions. 'We can't move off the pathways,' explains Director of Photography Russell Boyd, 'so the angles for shooting are difficult. And we're approaching like a guerrilla movement – with a much smaller crew.' The light, too, is different here and the methodology for utilising it old-fashioned. Everything has to be carried by hand, so reflecting what light they have is being done 'like D.W. Griffith did it in the old days – with a little shiny board.' Nor is there any alternative to climbing and lugging equipment up the steep hill on the island of Pinta – from which vantage point Stephen Maturin sees the dread *Acheron* and heralds the final conflict.

So every marine iguana, flightless cormorant, tortoise, fur sea lion and blue-footed booby caught by the camera is a creature of the Galapagos in its natural

environment. Finding animals to film isn't a problem: quite the opposite. 'They have no fear,' explains Mike Meehan. 'You can get really close; no need for a long lens. I nearly stepped on a marine iguana on my first visit. They're the same colour as the rock and they just lie there absorbing the sun. It's hysterical. They just lie around all day going "Aaah…." Then they slope off into the water. I guess they must have figured out they could feed off the algae so they learned to swim.' One can see why Stephen Maturin got so excited about going ashore at the Galapagos – and so apoplectic with rage at Jack for thwarting him and deriding his natural history 'hobbies'.

What is *not* shot in the Galapagos is the beach landing, the rescuing of the whalers, the crew's cricket match and the grisly sight of Maturin operating on himself. These are complex and time-consuming sequences involving many actors and a great deal of equipment. Exactly where to film was dictated in part by the need for a deep-water bay for the *Rose* and a terrain similar to the black lava of the Galapagos. For this, Mike Meehan had to look further afield, eventually finding a place near Todos Santos on the southern tip of Baja 'that literally translates as "get out if you can". The old road stopped abruptly,' he continues, 'and you had to bounce your way across rock for about eight hours to get there. Then you had to get out again the same way. But, for us, there's a huge bay there that's quite stunning. And the main point of it is that there's a small promontory full of lava very similar to where we were going to film on the Galapagos, so we decided to film our landing there.' The edited footage seamlessly intercuts the Galapagos Island footage with those scenes filmed in Mexico.

OPPOSITE *Tampering with tortoises – a sure sign that, unlike the above image, this scene was filmed at the Mexican 'stand-in' for the Galapagos Islands. Touching wildlife on the islands themselves is forbidden.*

# CHAPTER THREE

# Below the Decks

## BEHIND THE SCENES

The quickest way to get below decks on the *Surprise* is on a golf buggy, or – a favoured method on this set – by bicycle. If you're going to the gun deck either of those is preferable to walking because the deck is positioned rather incongruously on a bluff overlooking the sea at the edge of the studio complex.

The other sets – the great cabin; a portion of the orlop deck, the *Acheron* great cabin and the entire berthing deck – are inside on sound stages. The action in the film constantly moves from deck to deck and from exterior to interior: so, too, the schedule saw the crew moving from set to set. As Co-Producer Todd Arnow points out, 'The ship starts out looking a certain way, gets damaged, has to be repaired, gets dressed as a whaler, goes into battle and so on… the construction department has to deal with all that at the same time as we're trying to shoot the movie.' You can't 'dress' the ship whilst filming on it. You can't hang around. Cameras, like time and tide, wait for no man. They have to keep rolling as much

PREVIOUS SPREAD *The gun deck in the thick of battle.*

OPPOSITE *Jack Aubrey surveying the damage during the first encounter with the* Acheron.

*Down in the bilges trying to plug holes after the first encounter with the* Acheron. *This was filmed on a set on 'dry' land.*

*The berth deck where the men eat and sleep. Cramped and claustrophobic – and this is a film set. A 'real' berth deck would have had even lower deckheads. Again, this set is on dry land in the studio complex: on the tank ship there is nothing built below deck save a small section of the gun deck visible from above.*

as possible to get what, in the final edit, will amount to about one minute of screen time a day. So you have to find other places to film. But first you have to build them.

There are few concessions made for the camera below decks. The berth deck, for example, isn't built with the needs of a film crew in mind. In truth, it doesn't even look as if it's built with the needs of sailors in mind. It's claustrophobic and, with cast and crew inside, crammed to the gunnels (metaphorical gunnels, that is – real gunnels, or 'gunwhales', are the uppermost rails on the hull of a ship). Moreover, the berth deck and the gun deck are on gimbals again so, whilst on dry land, are capable of making you seasick.

*Seen here on the level, the gun deck has the facility to tilt thirty degrees to one side and twenty to the other.*

The deck is extremely impressive to look at, fascinating to be inside, awkward to film in and, one imagines, quite horrific to inhabit for any period of time. So it comes as a shock to learn that the beams, whilst not much more than 5 ft above the deck, have been made higher than would have been the case in O'Brian's *Surprise*. The extra height is a concession to filming requirements but, as Russell Crowe points out, 'you still can't stand upright. And that's

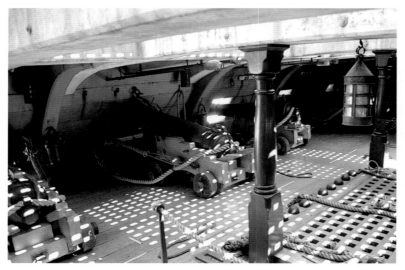

# HISTORICAL ADVISORS

'I want people to feel,' says Peter Weir, 'that this is as close as you can get to the impossible but exciting idea of travelling back to the past.' And to achieve that, the advisors became part of the fabric of life on this film. So much so that they were often dressed as extras, to be at hand, looking authentic, to advise on any last-minute detail.

They included Historical Consultant Gordon Laco, Armament Advisor Martin Bibbings, Swordmaster Dan Speaker, Sailing Master Andy Reay-Ellers and Master Shipwright Leon Poindexter.

Others who assisted include Brian Lavery of the National Maritime Museum, Peter Goodwin of the Victory Museum in Portsmouth, Mike Crumplin of the Royal College of Surgeons in England and Chuck Fithian, Curator of Archaeology at the Delaware Museum, who worked on the HMB *DeBraak* shipwreck.

Bringing lifetimes of experience in tall ships, tactics and technical aspects of 1805, these experts helped translate the reality of period life onto film. And the reality of O'Brian's characters: even the exact positioning of the scars to be placed on Jack Aubrey tallies with descriptions of wounds in the novels.

Most aspects of the film, from the authentic weave of the ships' lines to the buckles on the officers' shoes, were faithfully recreated.

And all the cast and many of the crew attended lectures about life in general, and in microcosm on the *Surprise*, in 1805.

The challenges faced by the team of specialists working on this production were immense. In the constant drive for authenticity in every aspect of the film, everything possible pertaining to the era was examined.

When history couldn't provide an answer, the solution was to provide history. At the time of writing, a live filming event using authentic materials is underway in order to produce – not approximate – the sound of the passage of ball, chainshot, grapeshot and barshot being fired. As Gordon Laco says, 'no one alive knows what they sounded like, so we have to find out for ourselves…'

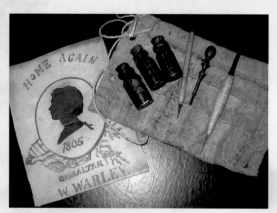

*Advisors were consulted on a wide range of subjects from the obvious to the arcane. The latter included eighteenth-century tattooing: here's the tattoo kit with Warley's silhouette from Gibraltar.*

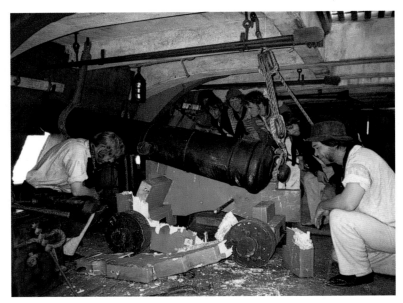

*The gun deck. The gun crews were drilled in exactly the manner they would have been in 1805. Records from gun crews of the time provided templates.*

something they didn't do in earlier films. If you look at *Damn the Defiant!* [HMS *Defiant* in the UK] or Errol Flynn films they didn't do that: their deckheads were about ten feet high.' As a result of their being considerably lower here, many of the film crew wore cycling helmets.

Gordon Laco, head man of the 'historical junta' of consultants, remarks that 'It's not true that they had low deck heads and so forth because the people were smaller. The average height was shorter than it is today, but not by much. The low headroom is actually a function of this ship's need to carry as big an armament as possible at a safe height above the waterline.' The configuration of the berth deck was, therefore, dictated mostly by the requirements of the gun deck above.

The hammocks, separated from each other by the standard fourteen inches, emphasise the appallingly cramped conditions. Yet having them in such close proximity carries a benefit that isn't immediately apparent. 'Running our own ships,' continues Laco, with reference to a lifetime working on tall ships, 'we discovered that if you spread the hammocks out they bang into each other when

*The officers in their ward room. A still life with input from props, costume, make-up and set-dressing.*

the ship rolls. If you keep them tightly together then they all sway together. It's not,' he concedes, 'what you'd choose…' Nor would one choose to sleep in what, in tropical climes, was a fetid hothouse with condensation from the men's bodies dripping off the beams.

Unlike the berth deck, the gun deck on the bluff benefits from natural light, which would have been the case had it been 'real'. The great cabin, again mirroring the real ship, is also part of this set. It also mirrors O'Brian's description of it in *The Far Side of the World*:

ABOVE *Hammocks on the berth deck were a regulation fourteen inches apart.*
BELOW *Jack Aubrey dines in the Great Cabin with his manservant Killick (David Threlfall) in truculent attendance.*

'…the noble great cabin, stretching clean across the ship and lit by the splendid, curved, inward-sloping, seven-light stern window, the airiest, lightest, most desirable place in the ship, Killick's kingdom, perpetually scoured, swabbed, scraped and polished, smelling of beeswax, fresh sea-water, and clean paint.' (O'Brian provides an amusing and pointed contrast to this with his next words: '"Perhaps we might have some music tonight?" suggested Stephen, coming up from his fetid dog-hole.')

ABOVE *This cannon is rigged for maximum elevation, with catspawed breeching ropes holding it in place.*
BELOW *Ship-shape and Bristol fashion when it's deserted, the gun deck looks entirely different with seven men per gun in the thick of battle.*

The great cabin is reproduced again, on its own, in an interior set which was used for filming more contained dialogue, dinner and musical scenes. Scenes that could actually have been filmed anywhere in the world because, as Todd Arnow says, 'we can strike and fold that set any time. We can travel with it. If it's needed for reshooting scenes after principal photography's finished, I can ship it anywhere in the world.' This wasn't, in the end, necessary, but as a contingency it exemplifies the need for forward planning.

The full gun deck on the bluff, with the facility to tilt thirty degrees to one side and twenty on the other, is utilised for cannon practice as well as for filming. The set itself is built, as ever, with accurate detail as the primary consideration. So are the cannons. And the gun crews are drilled in exactly the same manner as they would have been two centuries ago. 'It's like a ballet,' comments Martin Bibbings, the expert in eighteenth-century weaponry, who is responsible for training the crew. He's right: the twelve nine-pounders on either side of the deck have only 6 ft between them, and each has a crew of seven men, so every movement has to be minutely choreographed in order for the crew to load, take position, prime, aim and fire each weapon and then remove debris, clean the gun – and immediately repeat

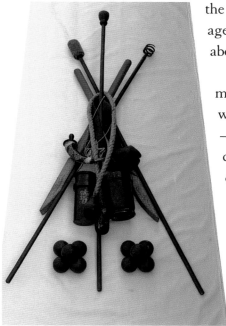

the procedure. The crews on the film have managed to fine-tune the whole process down to about fifty seconds.

As with elsewhere on the ship, the equipment that the actors and extras are dealing with are unfamiliar, and the constituent parts – rammers, swabs, wadhooks and the like – completely arcane. They are also authentic, down to the hand-painted *Surprise* standard on each of the powder horns. 'Everything,' says Bibbings, 'was specially made – some of it in India. No one in film has ever made weapons to this degree of accuracy... the recoil mechanism on these cannons, for example, is the best I have ever seen in my life, and all the cannons have flintlock igniters. *All* of them.' And that does mean all the cannons; there are no dummy ones. The only concession made for film was for ease of transportation: they're lighter than they would have been on O'Brian's *Surprise*.

Otherwise, they're faithful to O'Brian – right down to their names. 'The fact that each of the cannons has a name,' comments Gordon Laco, 'is down to O'Brian discovering from contemporary sailors' diaries that the guns were named by the crews that served them. So we've pounded through the books – and viewers will see that Jumping Billy and the rest are all here on this ship.'

In battle against the *Acheron* there are eighty-four gun crew amongst the cannons on the gun deck. If the ship had been unlucky enough to be sandwiched between two enemy vessels, the crew would divide onto both sides or would transfer from side to side between shots. It's not surprising that gun crews bled from their ears and noses: the noise would have been appalling. Additionally, to cause maximum carnage, gun captains used to try to make cannonballs bounce around the inside of enemy ships. Perhaps 'bounce' isn't the right word: one contemporary account reveals that a single cannonball sliced through twelve people.

*Wadhooks, rammers and swabs: all the constituent parts of the cannons, as well as the cannons themselves, were specially made for this production.*

*Flintlock igniters are rarely seen nowadays, but every cannon here has one.*

*Temperatures rising on the gun deck. The noise was deafening; sailors of the era often bled from their ears as well as their noses, and gun crews invariably became deaf.*

In the story's final battle, the *Surprise* topples the mast of the *Acheron* in order to cripple and board the ship. The *Surprise*'s guns, however, are too low to aim for the mast, so Jack orders Pullings to remove the rear wheels as well as everything else possible – wheels, quoin, bed and stool – in order to achieve a higher trajectory. 'The trouble there,' says Martin Bibbings, 'is that you then have the muzzle pointing out above the sill of the gun port. If you let the gun recoil, it'll take out a big, jagged hole above the port – so you have to cat's-paw the breeching rope, which literally ties the gun to the side of the ship, so that it can't recoil at all. It creates enormous strain – but that's how it was done.' And that's how they do it here. The tightness of the breeching ropes was vital anyway: they kept the cannons in place. And everyone knows the potential hazards of (yes, this is the origin of the term), a loose cannon…

Also on the gun deck is the Brodie stove, an astonishing feat of engineering used for cooking, but also helping keep the ship dry and warm. It's a direct descendant of the one found in the wreck of the *Pandora* – the ship that was carrying the mutineers from the *Bounty* back to England – off the coast of Northern Queensland. No one knew the dimensions of a Brodie stove, or indeed how to make one, until the stove from the *Pandora* was copied for the

ship *Endeavour*. This one, in turn, is based on that of the *Endeavour*. 'It was,' says Designer Marco Nero, 'the ultimate challenge. It was really difficult. Nobody knows all the details, but I made discoveries and tried to figure things out and did endless drawings. They were very, very happy with the results...' (The 'they' is a reference to the historical consultants who spend collective lifetimes immersed, variously, in eighteenth-century artefacts, weaponry and ships.) 'It's a different world. And it's a difficult balance: they know how to do ships; we know how to make movies. But Peter Weir blends everyone together. I'll tell you what's very, very nice,' adds Nero, 'Peter brings music all the time to the set. And to dailies [rushes in the UK]. That just charges everyone up, puts you in the mood for what you're doing. Music is very, very important.'

ABOVE *The guns above deck (right) are called carronades and have no wheels whilst cannons (left) lie below deck and look more traditional.*
BELOW *The ship's bell. A prop it may be, but it's historically accurate – and fully functional.*

Almost everyone in the cast and crew remarks on Peter Weir's playing of music – an eclectic range from Pink Floyd to Mozart – on set. Often very loudly. For soundtrack-searching, scene-setting, soul-lifting – even for pre-empting discord: everyone volunteers a reason. But it's the effect that's most interesting. Imagine preparing for a battle scene with a classical overture blasting through the gun ports...

Behind the scenes – behind those sets – is another creative enterprise at work: the Art Department. That department, together with the Props and Set Decorating departments, is responsible for everything from the look of the ships themselves to the painting on the powder horns.

## The Art Department

'Research,' says Supervising Art Director Bruce Crone. 'It's all about research. Constant research – and then more research.' Just in case one hasn't got the point, he gestures to an enormous pile of books in the aircraft-hangar-sized Art Department. *Marine Painting*, *Nelson's Battles*, *The Tall Ship in Art*, *Modèles Historiques* and *The 74-Gun Ship* are just a few – a very few – of the published sources from which this and every other department gleaned so much information.

Everything has to be drawn first. This is architectural practice as well as that of the Art Department. The construction drawings – thousands of them – have to be exactly to scale and precise in every detail: potentially difficult when one is unfamiliar with both the period and with nautical terms. 'You have to learn a different language,' says Bruce Crone. 'Dead-eyes, for instance… how can you design a dead-eye if you don't know what it is?' Well he does know now; he's been working on this production since the year before filming began, and talks with fluency and familiarity about davits, cleats and crosstrees as well.

*Assistant carpenter Nagle (Bryan Dick) at work mending the figurehead of the* Surprise. *Hundreds of construction drawings and sketches detail every stage of damage as well as of the building and repair process.*

That language aside, there's also French to contend with. There isn't much call for a translation of Jean Boudriot's *Modèles Historiques* which, as it transpires, isn't too much of a disaster as the principal rewards of this book are visual – down to pictures of restored model ships actually built in the eighteenth and nineteenth centuries. Models that even replicate, to the minutest detail, ship's interiors.

The pictures become potentially more confusing when one remembers the differing nationalities of the ships themselves. The *Acheron*, as recounted in the script, was American-built by, probably, English-trained shipwrights, but was substantially altered by the French. Look closely and you can see, for instance, the

Napoleonic 'N' on her. 'People who know the story will see the French aspects of that ship,' says Crone. 'There is,' for example, 'a French design to a knee and an English design to a knee.' (A knee, he explains, looks like 'a big corble' – which is no help whatsoever if you don't know what a corble is…) 'There are tiny differences,' he continues, 'between the two designs, so we had to be careful about that. We also had to be careful about remembering when our ships were built because there's a

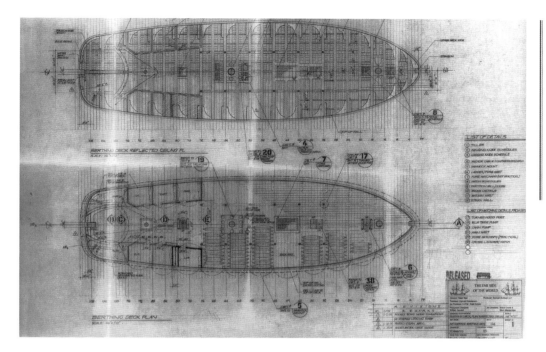

*Construction drawings of the berth deck (left) and the partition bulkheads and cabin doors (below). The tally of construction drawings for the whole production runs to many thousands.*

tendency to go beyond what you've seen and learned: you have to rein yourself in and remember reality.'

To give some idea of the sheer volume of construction drawings (that is, drawings done to exact scale), there are ninety-nine alone for where the standing rigging meets the channels on one side of the hull of the *Surprise*. There are at least ten of the *Acheron* figurehead, not including initial sketches. Incidentally, this figurehead is more like a billet-head and, purely coincidentally, the final design looked not unlike that on the USS *Constitution*...

Even before pre-production started in Baja, the Art Department was at work in Los Angeles, draughting drawings to convert the *Rose* (on which much of the rigging was actually too small) before cloning her for the *Surprise*. For the latter ship, two designers 'blocked' her, making a drawing for every twelve inches of

frame, manually scanning, in effect, something that didn't yet exist. Months later, in Baja, seventeen people are at work, designing, illustrating and storyboarding every aspect of the film. Every cannon is drawn here, as are Marco Nero's drawings for the binnacle box and the Brodie stove.

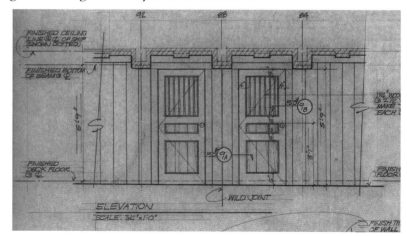

Here, too, is where every scene in the film is storyboarded. There are 378 scenes in this film. Whilst a picture may

*Storyboards of the raft built to act as a decoy for the* Acheron *and (far right), the* Acheron *firing at the raft, seen from the perspective of the deck of the* Surprise.

paint a thousand words, here it's the other way round. A scene may have dozens of accompanying storyboards, detailing every angle, character, wide-shot and close-up. They're drawn up sometimes months in advance, but they keep having to be altered – particularly on this film. Peter Weir is renowned for reacting to and running with unscripted nuances, often necessitating changes in subsequent storyboards. Storyboard Artist Christopher Buchinski remarks that 'he loves to run with the camera, which is amazing for a director. A lot of directors will nail down the area they're framing and not move the camera, but he loves to push the perspective beyond those lines.' Rather than being a nightmare, this, perhaps surprisingly, 'is just what a storyboard artist dreams of.' Then, remembering the reality, Buchinski adds 'We don't get enough sleep to dream...'

Changes of a different kind are vital pointers for the Art Department. The *Surprise*, for example, gets damaged, and that damage has to be drawn. 'We have to work out damage very specifically,' says Art Director Mark Mansbridge. 'It's especially important in a film like this.' He cites the example of the mast of the *Acheron*. The mast will only ever be seen as a jagged wreck (the full-rigging, as mentioned, is CGI'd), but they have to know *how*. Once they know, they can draw it accurately, with the damage 'based on the force and trajectory of the cannonball from the *Surprise* that hit it'. And that's a simple example. After the first encounter with the *Acheron*, the script describes the *Surprise* 'anchored fore and aft, leaning to larboard exposing her damaged side. A scaffolding has been rigged-up, and swarms with men, as does every part of this ship, including the rigging: 150 men and boys, hammering , sawing and splicing. Old Sponge and his son, both Greek ex-sponge divers, work at the stern, diving to repair the rudder pintles.' A colourful and industrious scene but, as with the subsequent close-up of Nagle repairing the splintered figurehead, all the damage has to be meticulously drawn, constructed and available for non-sequential shooting. 'That's why we have to look

ahead for action that's going to happen,' comments Bruce Crone. 'So as much as we can, we ask questions. If we don't do that,' he finishes, 'it makes us crazy and we want to run away.'

They wouldn't want to run next door, to the Set-Decorating Department, because that's where some of their drawings are realised. And if you ask questions there you get unexpected answers. 'Yeah,' says Bob Gould, 'I brought a team of four from Italy. Yeah… I know… Italy. I've worked on three films there and, believe me, they're very good craftsmen. I had incredible confidence in them.'

A well-placed confidence because much of what they made looks as if it came from museums. And all of it was handcrafted. 'Those lanterns,' says Gould, 'are hand-made. We made at least 250 of them. They're made of tin, pounded out in the old-fashioned way on an anvil. Saved me a lot of money as well… it does if you don't have things machine-made.'

*The Great Cabin of the* Surprise. *It was replicated down to the tiniest detail for both the model and the Computer Generated Image of the ship.*

# AUTHENTICITY AND ARTIFICE – VISUAL EFFECTS

*Master and Commander: The Far Side of the World* is a confluence of three worlds; a real one, a virtual one and a miniature one. On screen, they're seamlessly integrated. Dismantling them in prose seems almost subversive because it exposes the lie that viewers are always looking at a full-size ship. They're not. They are looking, sometimes alternately and sometimes simultaneously, at the full-size ship in Baja, at images generated entirely on computer, or at footage of miniature vessels constructed and filmed in New Zealand.

In the broadest possible terms, the miniatures were built because the *Acheron* in Baja is but a shadow of the ship it's supposed to be and the *Surprise* is stranded on its gimbal. Manoeuvring for battle, for example, is impossible, so it had to be done in miniature. And it was filmed in New Zealand because that's the base of Weta, the company that built the models (and, incidentally, did the visual effects for the *Lord of the Rings* films), and because those models are too large to ship to

the US. The 'miniature' of the *Surprise* is over thirty feet long. Asylum, a visual effects company in Santa Monica, is responsible for creating the digital (computer-generated) format.

Spotting computer generated images (CGIs) in the movie is pretty well impossible. 'Original' footage is scanned into the computer where artists work on it in a digital format before outputting it to film again. Other shots are generated in their entirety in the computer before being turned to film format. And CGI shots are dropped into scenes filmed in Baja (and in New Zealand) for a variety of reasons. The colour of the sea and the sky has to be changed to mirror the *Surprise*'s journey: wide shots need to be cropped because you don't want Baja or the lip of the tank in the background and, at almost every juncture, something has to be added. The view through the windows of the great cabin on the bluff at Baja, for example, is always computer generated. Even though one of the great cabin

*The* Surprise *without mast extension and (right) with plans for the computer-generated additions, with main topsail removed and topgallants and royals added.*

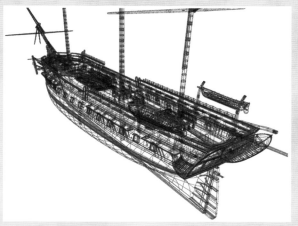 

*A high three-quarter view of the computer-generated wire-frame* Acheron *(left). A three-quarter view of the computer-generated* Acheron *created by CGI experts Asylum (right).*

sets overlooks the ocean, the scale was never right for filming purposes.

Much more fascinating than trying to extrapolate what shots may or may not be a CGI is the fact that the *Surprise* herself had to be computer generated. There is a digital model of this ship as well as a miniature one: a stand-alone entity contained in 3D form within a computer. As visual effects producer Helen Elswit points out, creating that ship was as difficult and painstaking as building the full-scale model. 'You cannot overstress how difficult a job that was. Lidar – a laser-scanning technology – was used to scan the *Surprise* for the computer, but that was just the start. All the blueprints created by the art department – and there were hundreds of them – were used for both the miniatures and the ships in the computer to finish all the detail on the ship: detail down to the lettering on the stern of the ship. Everything had to match *exactly*.'

Given that the final battle scene uses all three formats: miniature, computer-generated and footage filmed in Baja, one begins to get the picture. This is an interplay between miniature, virtual and 'real' – and to that end, even the people on those ships have to work in digital format. The computer work started after principal photography finished, but that didn't mean the Wardrobe Department could hang up their coats: people dressed in the correct outfits were scanned for the computer to create digital characters. 'You *must*,' says Helen Elswit, 'see people on both those ships.' (The digital and miniature versions of both the *Acheron* and the *Surprise*). 'They are for wider shots – they shot the closer shots in Baja – but, for continuity's sake, you have to be able to have both. You probably won't see the facial features but you'll be able to tell which are the French and which are the English.'

'That said,' continues Elswit, 'most of the film will have everything. The storm scene, the doldrums... they'll all be peppered, in some cases quite heavily, with CGI and miniature shots.' And again, everything on the miniatures and in the computer-generated ships has to match exactly to what's shot on film. There is absolutely no margin for error. To that end, countless e-mails and attachments wing their way, every day for months, between New Zealand and Santa Monica, adding what on paper seems a slightly surreal dimension to the movie.

BELOW *Taking the noon sight to give the best indication of a ship's latitude. Until 1805 (the year in which the film is set) a ship's day officially began at noon.*

The craftsmanship of the larger furnishings made here is remarkable: guns, swords, flags and all smaller items are, broadly speaking, under the remit of the Props Department. Again, research was the byword and historical advisors were on hand, but the authenticity also manifests itself in the care-worn look of some of the items. You wouldn't want to get too close to the hammocks, even when you realise the stains are made with coffee. 'The first guy I met here,' comments Gould, looking at them, 'knew where to buy hemp. You'd think they were made of canvas, wouldn't you? But they're not: they're made of hemp. And it's really difficult to find hemp in LA.' It's also really difficult to find hemp in Mexico – especially as the costume department needed acres of it as well for shirts and trousers. The best place to source it was, in fact, Pakistan. So that's where it came from. Gould's department used a substantial amount: they made 130 hammocks, as well as over 200 dummy hammocks for shots where they were seen rolled or stored.

They also made tables, benches, chairs, barrels and even a bellows – all of them to an exacting standard. A magnificent sea chest, one of 80 made for the officers and midshipmen, was copied from an original of the period, down to the last dovetail joint and the beckets (rope handles). The latter were made by Igor Bjorksten, an Australian rigger and technical advisor who used to work on the *Endeavour*. Officially, he was part of the rigging group on this project, but who better than a rigger, with years of experience with rope, knots and wood, to make those handles?

OPPOSITE *Each lantern was hand-made on set from beaten tin. No mass-production here.*

## Costumes

'We managed to get hold of this guy, a cordwainer… that's a shoemaker… who located these shoes from a ship that had sunk in 1806. With the water being so cold, the shoes were very well-preserved. He took photographs and from those he made a last and some samples. We okayed them,' finishes Costume Supervisor Jim Tyson, 'and from them we modelled every single pair of shoes on this picture.' About 1900 pairs of shoes. And if you want Jim Tyson to expound on the finer points of that footwear, he'll show you innumerable books, drawings and paintings of the period and elaborate on the differences between the shoes worn by the French and the English. Generalities like the fact that there was no right

*Midshipmen, marines, seamen and whalers: an example of the huge array of costumes designed and made for this movie.*

and left 'hand' for the footwear: specifics such as the gradual replacement, for younger English naval officers of the time, of buckles with laces. And for those who stuck with buckles, the production had them made by an English firm who knew what they were doing because they have been doing it since 1794.

The same breadth of research and depth of knowledge applies to even smaller items, like buttons. All the buttons for this film were made by a button-caster in London who has also been operating since the 1770s. Even tiny details got the similar treatment. The cockade of the hat belonging to the captain of the *Acheron* has a type of ribbon that is only made in Japan: no other type of ribbon currently available on this planet can do the job of making that cockade so authentic. There are people who notice things like that. And for those who miss them, that's fine by Tyson. 'If you don't notice the clothes, if you're not going "Oh, look at that" then it means we did a good job.'

In addition to the shoes, the Costume Department, headed by Wendy Stites, made nearly three thousand costumes and two thousand hats. Hundreds of books were consulted for reference, and the National Maritime Museum in London became a central axis of research. From further afield, over fifteen thousand yards of fabric from countries including China, Pakistan, Italy and India

*The Master Allen (Robert Pugh) in one of the hats knitted in Wales specifically for this production – to the same design and using the same type of wool as was used two hundred years ago.*

were used. The knitted caps worn by English sailors were made by a lady in Wales whose family have been spinning and weaving with wool made by her family for the past two hundred years. The hemp for the shirts and trousers was again sourced in Pakistan but was nearly lost when the courier found not fabric but a sign at the manufacturer's saying 'Closed for a funeral. Don't know when I'll be back'. And Chinese New Year delayed another shipment by four weeks.

So costumes are big business. They're also extremely complex. Establishing correct period details, from head to toe, for several hundred people was the major priority. Homage to Patrick O'Brian was another: 'Peter Weir had made costume notes about the characters from his reading of the books, so we incorporated as many as we could,' says Tyson. 'They helped with establishing individuality and eccentricities.' The coat that Maturin wears on the Galapagos is a good case in point. 'The banyan, an Indian fabric,' says Tyson, referring to the coat, 'is one of his eccentricities. It's like him saying "This is my bush coat". It looks great on camera…'

That's another vital consideration for the Costume Department: authenticity has to sit within the parameters of cinematography. The shirts worn by the whalers imprisoned in the *Acheron* look, in the light of day, perfectly filthy: much dirtier than they appear on camera. But even though they're filmed, darkly, in the bowels of the ship, they still appear whiter than they really are. 'One of the problems with hemp is that it's difficult to age,' says Tyson. 'And white things that you age up always come out whiter than they really are.'

Everything here is custom-made for this production, yet it has to be made to look as if it's been knocking about at sea for ages; that alone accounts for several thousand man-hours. Tyson greets a question about why costumes aren't hired with a slightly bemused look. 'Well, there hasn't been a production

*The coat that Stephen Maturin wears on the Galapagos Islands is a banyan, commonly worn by people who had travelled widely.*

anything like this in… decades? And, anyway, if you hire things you have to be responsible for damage to them. This is a five-month production. One of the reasons why we get through so many pairs of shoes is that they wear through them. Russell Crowe alone has twelve pairs of boots…' He adds that, with twenty-five principal actors constantly in uniform, it's inconceivable not to have them tailor-made – and that the officers of the period would anyway have had bespoke uniforms.

Ageing costumes is a curious process involving both the arcane and the obvious. The aforementioned shoes and boots tend to take care of themselves when the actors and extras are playing baseball. 'We like them doing that,' laughs Tyson. 'It means we don't have to age them.' And, yes, in the past he has used that highly sophisticated ageing method: tying them to the backs of trucks and dragging them along the ground.

Clothes have to be lovingly tended to achieve the patina of age and wear but not, as Tyson points out, of Dickensian raggedness. 'It's quite well documented that one day each week was set aside for washing and repairs. They took good care of their things, and the men became pretty good at sewing. They made nice things and they made interesting things. And they made use of what they had and what they brought on board at different ports. That's why you see seamen with shirts made of the same cloth in the film… stripy cloth… checked cloth… they used what they had.'

The men on the *Surprise* would be at sea for up to two years on this voyage. They had very little to call their own, so it stands to reason that, for the most part, they would take pride in what they did possess. Especially the officers. There are contemporary accounts revealing that they could be quite competitive about the origin and quality of everything from their epaulettes to their boots. As mentioned, all were custom-made for each individual, and their choice of cloth and tailor was one of the few visible manifestations on board ship of their wealth. Ed Woodall (Mowett) probably scores the most points here. His top coat was made from a cloth personally selected by ex-President Gorbachev of Russia a month before he was removed from office. For some mysterious reason, it had been hanging around at a London tailor's for the last ten years.

It takes longer to distress the clothes than it does to make them. Dyes and textile paint and Fuller's Earth are used. Salt is rubbed into jackets. (One actor was surprised to find a small rock in the pocket of his jacket one day. It hadn't got there by accident: Wardrobe had placed it there in order to spoil the line of the cut.)

*Sailors' attire could be extremely varied. They often made their own clothes, from old sails as well as from material purchased at ports of call all over the world.*

First Lieutenant Pullings (James D'Arcy) shouting orders. Note he wears his hat fore and aft, not, like Jack Aubrey, in the manner of Nelson (overleaf).

Talcum powder is heat-sealed into some fabrics. Blowtorches take the newness out of wool. Sandpaper, de-natured alcohol and glycerine are part and parcel of the process. Collars of hemp shirts are attacked with implements that look like cheese-graters. And most clothes receive a good stonewashing before they're dyed, in order to remove the sheen. Almost all the fabric had to be washed before it was turned into clothes. These are all natural fibres and some of them shrink by as much as thirty per cent on their first washing. Interestingly, most of the gold used on stitching and for some buttons aged itself. Gold oxidises quickly and turns green, especially when exposed to the elements. 'We didn't want to go for a Gilbert & Sullivan, shiny *Pirates of Penzance* look,' says Tyson.

It took longer for the Costume Department to distress the clothes than it did to make them.

Not 'standing out' isn't confined to gold; it's a general prerequisite. And on film it can be a problem when it comes to red. 'It's a very tricky colour,' says Tyson. 'If you use red, you really have to mean it. The Marines have to have it, but otherwise we've saved it for the French.' The overall look, he emphasises, is more 'spots of colour' than kaleidoscopic. The red on the Marines' uniforms was muted to avoid looking

too bright on camera and to complement and not glaringly counterpoint the royal blues. 'And we're using a grey-blue for some of our seamen. When you see the movie I think you'll understand why I think Wendy's colour palate is one of the best I've seen for a movie like this.'

Perhaps surprisingly, the Marines' uniforms were the only clothes that, of the period, were extremely regimented. Red coats with blue trousers in winter and white ones in summer and – this is one of the first films to show these – an 'undress' uniform of a shorter jacket in white and, overseas, a forage cap. Naval uniforms in the early nineteenth century were rather more fluid. Indeed, the concept of a 'uniform' only evolved in the mid-eighteenth century, and only applied to commissioned officers and midshipmen. Officially, they were introduced in 1748 and were inspired, according to a charming but probably apocryphal legend, by the Duchess of Devonshire's riding habit of a blue coat with white lapels. Yet more than fifty years later, captains still paid for some of their crew to be dressed smartly, according to their choice. In 1820, the captain of HMS *Harlequin* dressed his gig crew up as… harlequins.

No such eccentricities for Jack Aubrey. The uniforms of his officers and midshipmen can trace their antecedents straight back to the National Maritime

*Marines were known as 'lobsters' due to the colour of their coats. Like the stiff stocks worn by the officers, the leather collars they wore helped the actors in their roles: they invite a rigid posture.*

Museum in England (where the uniform Nelson died in is on display). Aubrey's slightly old-fashioned breeches are modelled on Nelson's, with stocking showing just below the knee. 'Yes, it looks odd if you think about it,' says Tyson, 'but Russell was more than happy to wear them.' Other actors wore the more modern pantaloons, and here personal preferences were part of the equation. Again, it was a question of feeling comfortable as well as looking the part. In the colder-climate scenes, the fact that the officers wear different types of overcoat is no accident. 'Uniform' coats were incredibly expensive, and many officers co-opted their 'civilian' coats into use rather than add to their expenses.

Fundamentally, not that much has changed about Royal Naval uniforms. Officers still wear navy blue with epaulettes. And black scarves, jumper-type shirts and bell-bottom trousers are still worn. Shirts for the film were manufactured from patterns straight out of historical books. These have the tight shoulder-cut of the time rather than the more flamboyant, flapping-sleeve look favoured in fiction. 'They're not very comfortable for the actors,' says Tyson, 'but they're straight out of the period. Maybe we have kept them a bit more "uniformed" than normal,' he continues, 'but apart from the Galapagos, we never go on land. And the important thing for us is to tell them apart from the French privateers at the end – to know who's who.'

*Marines on parade. Their red coats provided vivid colour in an otherwise carefully muted production.*

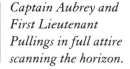

*Captain Aubrey and First Lieutenant Pullings in full attire scanning the horizon.*

'The extraordinary thing about the costumes on this film,' says James D'Arcy (Pullings) 'is that simply to put them on is in some way to become the character. They're incredibly constricting. They make you stand up straight, particularly if you have to wear an officer's uniform. And they make you feel like a gentleman. That's sort of half the battle won.' One gets some idea of just how peculiar they must be to wear on discovering that none of the trousers have pockets, and the uniforms, heavy in the first place, are almost unbearably so when soaking wet – and not much better in the searing heat.

Ed Woodall (Mowett), echoes D'Arcy's words, adding that the uniforms injected some much-needed elegance in him. 'I'm a bit of a scruff-bag normally. I've got quite a reputation around here for being the worst-dressed actor… in fact the worst-dressed person on the whole shoot. I really frighten people sometimes… So the uniform really makes me stand nice and tall. I feel good in it. I feel good with the stock round my neck. The hat,' he adds, 'is a little more difficult to get to grips with. Especially the fore and aft one – in fact it's caused a lot of problems on set. It's so *big*. I don't know why, but it seems much bigger than James's. I've had my hat on and Peter has said "We can't see anything. We can't see any of the other actors – his hat's in the way." To counteract that problem it was decided that Pullings would be seen more often in a fore and aft hat whilst Mowett would usually sport a top hat. 'I found that very odd,' says Woodall. 'A top hat?'

*First Lieutenant Pullings (James D'Arcy, left) and Second Lieutenant Mowett (Ed Woodall, right) flank their captain on the quarterdeck. The length and abundance of sideburns was a matter of personal choice – for officers as well as seamen. Officers were often competitive about the latest fashions in uniforms.*

But other elements of his costume were still determined to grab attention. 'My big blue coat,' he grins. 'It's the "Gorbachev" one, made from a kind of special mohair material – very special as it turned out. It changed colour: it went purple in the storm…'

Like other actors on set, Woodall was impressed, surprised and sometimes even alarmed by the costume choices. 'Like with the top hat, I initially thought the coat was totally inappropriate: I thought "That's a pantomime coat" – but, of course, it wasn't. They've made some wonderful decisions with the costumes, you know. You start off thinking "can we really get away with that?" and then you realise these things are researched and they actually work on camera. But,' he concedes, 'no one actually knew my coat was going to turn purple with all the sea-water being sprayed at us…'

An unplanned and highly visible feature, then. But most other elements of costume are planned to the last detail – even if they are invisible. Nagle's accessories, for example. Bryan Dick, who plays the part of the carpenter's mate, went through every aspect of his character with Peter Weir, discussing everything from his appearance to the accoutrements that he would carry with him as he went about his business on board the ship. Little of this is for the benefit of the camera: it's all about *being* Nagle rather than looking like a carpenter's mate. 'I have Nagle's things. I have a little pouch with chisels, I've got a little knife. I've got my apron and everything. It's strange,' muses Dick, 'but, knowing that I've got my little chisels there, kind of helps my character.'

Tony Dolan, playing his boss, carpenter Mr Lamb, has even more accessories, 'Including a thrum cap,' says Dolan. 'I found out about it from my researches. It's not the prettiest thing in the world, but it's exactly right – and it's a hat that nobody's ever worn before on a film. There have been,' he adds with a wry grin, 'a lot of comments about it here. But it's interesting: apparently all carpenters wore these hats so that when there was a lot of activity every single

*Assistant Carpenter Nagle (Bryan Dick, left) had more than clothes to fit his character: he also had accoutrements including chisels and knives to help him play his part.*

person on board could spot the carpenter.' Nodding at the woolly, brown and, in close-up, deeply unattractive little number, he corroborates what his colleagues have said about slipping into costume and therefore into character. 'It's funny, it just helps… I walk onto the set as a carpenter.'

Of his shirt, Dolan reveals an equally fascinating history. When he first arrived in Baja, Wendy Stites showed him a piece of the material which 'she actually found in an old Australian prison. Apparently this material was given to the convicts to wear as a uniform. It was originally for sailors, it was cheap and they had loads left over so they gave it to convicts. Wendy had it replicated so, again, it helps. I know it's from the period.'

In some scenes, both Joe Morgan (Warley) and Tony Dolan (Lamb) wear a caterpillar jumper – a forerunner of today's T-shirt – but of knitted wool. For Warley, as captain at the mizzen mast, it has different advantages. 'It's made so that it can be tucked out of the way and make it really easy for me to climb the mast and deal with the ropes. I had a great day near the beginning with Wendy,'

*Ship's carpenter Mr Lamb (Tony Dolan) wearing the shirt made from material matching that found by Costume Designer Wendy Stites in an old Australian prison.*

he remembers. 'I came in and she said my costume was far too clean, so we got out the mud and the scissors, ripping it and tearing holes in the top to match the wear and tear of the jobs I do. Then they had to copy the exact same holes with about ten shirts. You know, shirts for being wet and shrunken in the water and everything...'

'You might think,' says Robert Pugh (The Master Allen) of the Costume Department, 'that these people come and stick a costume on you and push you onto the set. They don't. They check their references, photographs and notes, and tell you whatever you want to know about what you're going to be doing. It's amazing. And I've got this wig,' he adds, stroking his locks. 'This famous, fantastic wig. I've had long hair before but I haven't had long *grey* hair before... it *so* helped the character. Suddenly there he is: I just look in the mirror and see Master Allen.'

Hair may be big in this movie but hats are bigger – much bigger. There are over 2000 in all, and Production Milliner Susan Anderson made about 1500 of them. One of the greatest headwear concerns was the quality of the felt. When you age poor-quality felt it begins to acquire a cardboard look, but there's nothing pauper-like about the felt used for Jack Aubrey's hats: 'We managed to get the last six flushes of

*Jack Aubrey drenched on the quarterdeck. The heavy woollen uniforms almost doubled their weight when soaked.*

*Warley (Joe Morgan, left) in his stripey jumper – a fore-runner of today's T-shirt – made of knitted wool. Initially far too clean, it was aged with the help of mud and scissors.*

this incredible quality from Italy,' says Tyson. 'There aren't any more. We got terribly excited about that. Especially as we had to fight another film to get them…'

Whilst the woolly hats of the English seamen look simple, more complex, or perhaps foppish, are those of the French privateers – in particular that of the French captain. This is a man about whom we know nothing, but whose menacing presence is felt throughout the film. There had to be something sinister about

*The Master Allen (Robert Pugh) in yet another hat. There was an official coat for officers to wear at sea, but many had just one for both land and sea – expense was often the primary concern here.*

him. There is: his hat, with black, hand-dyed and only slightly distressed feather. A suggestion, if you will, of the ominous black swan. His coat, too, stands out. It has a rather outrageous, foppish collar with magnificent piping and gold leaf. A glimpse is all we get on film, but it's all that's needed to suggest that he's some-one out of the ordinary.

From a filmic point of view on board the *Surprise*, hats look great but, as Jim Tyson points out, 'we pay a lot of money for these actors. And we have a lot of close-ups so you have to be careful with hats. Sometimes we lose them because we

*Hollom's funeral at sea. A not very appropriate (but rather opportune) moment to see some of the thousands of yards of hemp used by the Costume Department.*

*The Costume Department didn't want a shiny gold look for the officers' uniforms. Fortunately, the ageing process occurred naturally with the gold – seen here in Jack Aubrey's epaulettes – oxidising itself when exposed to the wind and the water.*

want to see the actors' faces.' But creativity in this area flourished in, colour-wise, the most vivid, vibrant scene of the film – the landing in Brazil. This scene was impeccably researched. Brazilians on the coast did indeed wear a motley, eclectic collection of outfits, mostly inspired by their years of contact with European traders. Hard evidence of this is found in photographs – albeit of a slightly later period – of native Brazilians dressed in top hats and carrying umbrellas. Some of the costume ideas were inspired by these and, as Tyson says, 'We had a lot of fun doing the Brazilians. We had forty people to do. Wendy and I went to a place in LA where they had boxes and boxes full of ancient lace and aprons, old parasols and things. We tacked things on to those and also made necklaces and loincloths. What was really strange was going on-line and finding this woman who went into the jungle

*Nearing land. The scenes off the coast of Brazil add a blaze of colour – and a load of supplies – without detracting from the plot.*

in Brazil once a year and got these amazing feathers and beads and things. It was amazing… we thought we might have to go to the Amazon or something but we did an internet search and found her.' It lends a whole new dimension to Amazon on-line.

Back in Baja, filming is sometimes not so much fun. For the Costume Department, it's a sixteen-hour day, seven days a week, mending, stitching – and washing. Everything is washed at least every two days. There are launderers working throughout the night, every night, using a combination of baking soda

*More than a few lingering looks were cast in this direction. There are no women on board (unless you count Aspasia the goat. And as revealed in O'Brian's* The Far Side of the World, *one seaman did…)*

and light soap so it doesn't remove the distressing. And the manufacturing process continues during filming as well. For the final battle scene and with the influx of about 150 new extras and stuntmen, new clothes had to be made. 'Sometimes,' says Tyson, 'we're actually grabbing extras, taking their shirts off and giving them to other people who are on-camera. You see, they do a take and might decide to do it

again because they didn't like the way a certain bullet hit. Well, the shirt can't be used again because we're using squibs and blood and everything…'

But Tyson's biggest problem comes from a more surprising source. 'The kids are growing out of their clothes. The powder monkeys' feet have grown two sizes throughout the summer and Lord Blakeney's just outgrown everything…'

# Make-up & Hair

Portraits of the era were essential parts of the research process here, yet working from these images invariably carries a caveat. Few people would have consented to having their portrait painted on a 'bad hair day'. And often, especially in the past, a portrait was intended to portray a stylised ideal rather than reality. Henry VIII, after all, married Anne of Cleves on the strength of her rather charming portrait – and promptly divorced her, it is said, on account of the rather hideous reality. A century later, however, Oliver Cromwell was credited with coining the expression 'warts and all' by insisting that his portrait be as true a likeness as possible, with blemishes painted in rather than out.

Hair Department Head Yolanda Toussieng is all too aware of the potential pitfalls of mirroring the glorious grooming of portraiture. Yes, she studied portraits and sketches of the time, but 'an essential part of what we do in research is to find out exactly what hair knowledge there was at the time. What did a hairdresser in 1805 know? What did he use for cutting and styling hair? So we also studied the combs, razors and wigs recovered from sunken ships of the period.' Written accounts helped here, too, and Patrick O'Brian's writing, attentive to the minutiae of daily life on board ship, provides snapshots of sailors grooming their own and their compatriots' hair.

The popular image of the Navy as a floating hell populated by unkempt wretches is, once again, at odds with reality as regards personal grooming. Sailors did spend time tending to their own and each others' appearance and they were required to shave twice a week, although, as Russell Crowe points out, the reality must at times have been different from that regulatory ideal. 'Shaven and pink-cheeked may have been how they presented themselves to the Admiralty – but in bad weather off the north coast of Brazil? You can't get up and run cold steel across your face no matter what the weather; the movement of the sea would preclude that. You'd be cutting your throat.' It's a good point, borne out of experience: you can regulate everything about the Navy except the one thing that keeps it afloat – the sea.

But within the man-made regulations, fashion, status and personal preference all played their parts. Most of the actors, personally, would have preferred not to have a

*'Shaven and pink-cheeked may have been how they presented themselves to the Admiralty…' says Russell Crowe. In the aftermath of battle, grooming is the last thing on anyone's mind – but the first for those in Make-up and Hair.*

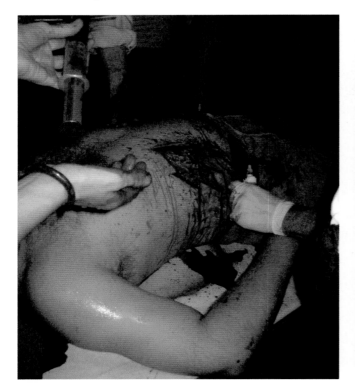

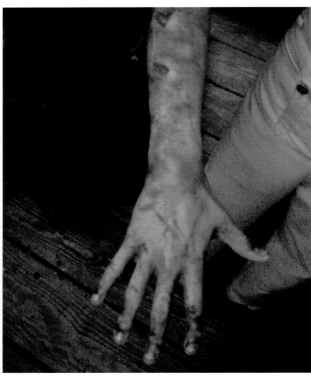

*Blood flowed quite freely on this production – extracted (left) from syringes and, happily, not from the actors' internal organs. Right: Midshipman Blakeney's gangrenous hand is photographed for continuity purposes.*

mullet haircut and itchy sideburns – but that was the prevailing fashion. Given that neither beards nor moustaches were permitted, those who wanted facial hair were limited to sideburns – in some cases, enthusiastic, bristly ones. Yet 1805 wasn't a particularly hirsute period, and although all the actors were asked not to cut their hair between casting and filming, this wasn't necessarily to do with length. The look decided by Peter Weir and the requests of the actors themselves were all taken into account, but, as Yolanda Toussieng explains, 'Even if they've had a haircut within the last few months you can tell that the technology used wasn't that of 1805.' This may seem quite extreme, but Toussieng is adamant that any vestiges of a modern haircut would be spotted in front of the camera. 'Today's cuts have distinct lines in them. In 1805 they used razors to cut their hair: the scissors on board ships were mainly used to cut cloth, not hair.'

Given that 120 people went to the hairdresser every day for five months on this set, practicality and time-constraints played a huge part in the process. Of the principal cast of twenty-five, only five wore wigs and three had hair extensions. Wigs are terrifically time-consuming, and most people don't like wearing them anyway. Hair extensions, once in place, are relatively hassle-free and can be treated like real hair. Indeed they *are* made of real hair, glued, heated and melted into the actors' own hair. It takes about fifteen hours to dress one head of hair, but extensions wear well, and it's a process that only had to be repeated once during the whole production.

When it comes to make-up, authenticity is achieved in a different way. The very nature of the subject matter precludes the need to emulate cosmetic treatments of the day: sailors didn't wear make-up but they did 'wear' scars, and, in battle, liberal amounts of blood. As regards the latter, Department Head Ed Henriques says, 'I've worked with Peter before, but I've seen a new side to him on this film. He's often calling for more blood so we gave him his own bottle in the end. We called it Peter Weir's Kensington Gore.' But quash any images of the director rampaging around spraying blood all over his actors: this is an example of meticulous attention to detail. Most of this personal supply was used for set-dressing. A little extra smear on a beam; a small bloodied trace of fingerprints on the wooden walls of the gun deck… touches reflecting the constantly evolving nature of filming this production.

Blood aside, one of the fundamental aspects of make-up in this movie is to make people who spent five months in Baja look as if they were travelling huge distances through vastly differing climates. It helped that, whilst filming wasn't done in continuity, scenes of extreme weather conditions were, by and large, filmed *en bloc*. A less forgiving schedule might have obliged the make-up department to 'weather' 120 people for the equator one day and for the Antarctic the next – and then revert to the equator again the following day.

*Flesh wounds from hand-to-hand combat and flying splinters resulted in blood everywhere.*

Do these things matter very much? Will people really notice the skin tones of the seamen? Yes. People generally don't notice if things look right. But anachronisms can jar on any level, however small – an extreme example is a website dedicated to a continuity slip-up in the growth of Kate Winslet's nails in the movie *Titanic* (sad, but true). The point – as Jim Tyson explained about the costumes – is for nothing to stand out. A great deal of thought went into how the characters themselves would look at different points throughout the film. 'When they were in the cold going round the Cape,' says Ed Henriques, 'we wanted a blotchiness to reflect that: bits of red on noses and on the earlobes. Then, when they were in the doldrums, we gave them red sunburn lines and red foreheads. We wanted redness there so that we could save the brown for when they were coming up to the Galapagos.' Little elements, barely noticeable; but beautifully realised.

More pertinent to the action element of the film are the visible manifestations of that action: the characters' scars. And here it's not just a familiarity with the script that's required in make-up, but knowledge of Patrick O'Brian's books. A description of Pullings' lengthy scar on his forehead, for example, is found in O'Brian. Some characters requiring minor mutilation were played by actors (decorum prevents Henriques from naming names, but one of them is Ed Woodall) who had scars of their own that make-up enhanced but most – and there

*Scenes of extreme weather conditions – blisteringly hot (above) and freezing cold (opposite) – were largely filmed en bloc. Otherwise it means 'weathering' 120 people for the equator one day and for the Antarctic the next – and then revert to the equator the following day.*

*Lieutenant Pullings (James D'Arcy) undergoes a little light mutilation as his prominent scar is touched-up on set.*

# TATTOOING

Ever since Captain Cook ventured to the South Pacific, the art of tattooing has been linked closely with the lives of sailors. Whilst the first tattoos were done by native Polynesians, sailors soon began to tattoo each other aboard ship, and the practice spread quickly throughout the Royal Navy and then to other navies, with former sailors often establishing tattoo parlours in port cities throughout the world. In 1789 Captain Bligh of the *Bounty* recorded that, of the twenty-five mutineers, eighteen had tattoos – including Fletcher Christian who had a star 'tattowed [sic] on his left breast'. A century later it was estimated that ninety per cent of all sailors in the US Navy had tattoos.

Of the infinite varieties of design, there were many that were standard and, reputedly, had specific meanings. In the movie, Joe Plaice has 'Hold' tattooed on one knuckle, and 'Fast' on the other – a fairly common tattoo at the time, which was said to help sailors climb the rigging. But most tattoos were pictorial: an anchor showed that the seaman had sailed the Atlantic Ocean; a fully-rigged ship was supposed proof of sailing round Cape Horn; and a dragon demonstrated that a seaman had served on a China station.

Other tattoos were more personal. The ever-growing chain around Awkward Davies' torso is (according to Awkward Davies and you don't want to argue with him) a link-for-link tally of the men he has killed in battle, although as actor Alex Palmer (Slade – who has an octopus tattoo) says, 'Obviously sailors do tell very tall stories. This looks like one of them…' On the other hand, Patrick O'Brian's Davies is violent, brutal and, according to Jack, a 'cannibal', so one cannot be too sure… The full chain, whilst taking 'only' around three hours to recreate in make-up, would have been a long, painstaking and painful process and, appropriately, is used in the movie as a device to denote the passage of time.

*Slade (Alex Palmer) applies the next link to Awkward Davies (Patrick Gallagher). Slade was the ship's unofficial tattooist: Davies was the unofficial madman. Each link, he claimed, represented a man he had killed.*

are a lot of scars and wounds from splinters and hand-to-hand combat – had to be applied. So, too, did the tattoos sported by a few of the characters, most notably Awkward Davies with an ever-growing chain around his torso. And as for the designs of the tattoos, Henriques points out that 'None of these people, obviously, are around any more and there are no photographs, so it's really speculative as to what designs the sailors would have for tattoos.' But again there are surviving references to hand that can help: 'I found that scrimshaws [carved bones, shells or ivory] were the best source of art the sailors did at the time. So I had a lot of tattoos designed from tiny scrimshaws of the time.' And where sailors led, others followed: tattoos became quite popular in the West following Captain Cook's journey to Polynesia. The word itself has roots in both the Tahitian and Marquesan languages.

Another basic of make-up on set is that, contrary to 'real' life, its parameters here extend to dirt. But not much. As mentioned, sailors could be quite fastidious about their appearance; indeed the Royal Navy at the time was much envied by foreign sailors for its standards of hygiene. 'But,' says Henriques, 'it occurred to me that there was no running water and the tar they used to prevent water-damage was everywhere. We'd think of it more as a resin, but it was tar – so there it would tend to get everywhere, especially beneath the sailors' fingernails.' So a coating of greyish powder mixed with a binder is applied to fingernails, in the lines around the eyes and on cracks in skin. As with dirt on clothes, it has to be exaggerated to show on camera, so at close quarters some of these sailors look rather unappetising. They actually look as if they should smell.

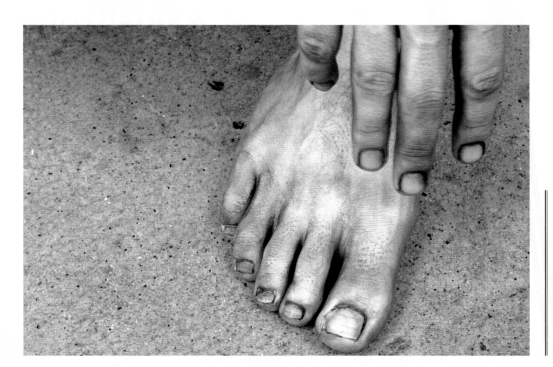

*Manicures and pedicures are rather different on this movie. Fine lines, fingernails and feet were all coated with a greyish powder mixed with binder to achieve that tar-covered look.*

Whilst much time is spent on getting looks right, this, paradoxically, invites an anachronism. Sure, you can't help but look in a mirror when you're in make-up but, as a general principle, gazing at one's reflection has been discouraged on this production from the very beginning. This wasn't to quell narcissistic tendencies but was due to period considerations. These men didn't get up in the morning and look at themselves in a mirror. They lived two hundred years ago; they were on a crowded ship and they were at war. And they had no water on tap. The actual extent to which each individual did or didn't care about his personal appearance has to be a matter of conjecture, but it's a matter of fact that they simply didn't have the wherewithal to indulge in lengthy bouts of personal grooming. It's probably true to say that most of them, on a day-to-day basis, didn't even know what they looked like.

Ed Henriques cites the analogy of a contemporary camping holiday as an aid to experiencing how these men actually lived. 'It occurred to me that it may have been similar to us going camping for a week or two. You know, you try to wipe things off and stay clean as best you can – so that's what we were going for here.'

'It's odd,' says Ed Woodall, having unwittingly used the same analogy, 'if you spend a week without looking at yourself at all. It's quite a weird thing. We don't think about it because we get up in the morning and one of the first things anyone does is look in the mirror and brush their teeth or whatever. These guys didn't. I don't suppose they really knew how dirty they were.'

*Ed Woodall as Second Lieutenant Mowett. 'I'm a bit of a scruff-bag normally. I've got quite a reputation for being the worst-dressed person on the whole shoot.' But not whilst in uniform. 'It really makes me stand nice and tall.'*

Bryan Dick relates with amusement that the actors, despite the caveat about mirrors and therefore self-awareness, know exactly how dirty they are. 'We turn up every day and get covered in filth. Basically, that's how the make-up works. We have filth under our nails, filth around our nails. Our arms are filthy. We've sunburned, they put extra tan on us and then they cover us in mud, basically.'

A slight exaggeration, maybe, but even at the beginning of the movie the men have been at sea for months. They've long been accustomed to the omnipresent tar and to sporting two-day stubble. Their hairstyles, however, were dictated by the 'look' of the day as well as by their environment. Yolanda Toussieng points out that midshipmen were generally groomed to look like captains and that many of them would have had the fashionable 'Napoleon' hairstyle as epitomised by Mowett. 'It has to be brushed forward and then curled,' says Woodall, seemingly quite chuffed at his transformation from scruff-bag. Of the ministrations of Ed Henriques, he's absolutely delighted. 'He's a wonderfully subtle make-up artist.' Then he gestures to his lusciously primed sideburns. 'These are my pride and joy. Ed works them every day, waxing them and pulling them forward so that they have these little tendrils. Nothing too flashy, but just making them look as if this is the way they grow naturally. It was very fashionable.

James D'Arcy, sporting Pullings's prominent scar on his cheek, relates the research and development behind it. 'It's described quite vividly in the books – it's from a sabre slash. Ed Henriques had used this amazing technology to put it on a photograph of me, to show me when I arrived. It was monstrous; so distracting that I thought you'd have been able to see nothing but the scar. Then he showed me some other ideas that he'd had, and he'd made it a little subtler but still interesting – in fact I think *more* interesting. It's more curly now, you know,' he adds, stroking the silicone graft. 'You can really feel how that sabre might have just swiped across the face there. I'm really happy with it. I think,' he finishes, demonstrating the fine line in wry British humour, 'that it's quite beautiful actually.'

*Getting it in the neck. A particularly gruesome testament to sword-slashing make-up skills. This poor fellow plays a French sailor (but not for very long) on the* Acheron.

*Hair extensions come in bundles: real hair glued, heated and melted into the actors' own hair. Department Head Yolanda Toussieng (right) has used more than four hundred bundles of hair on this production.*

# DENTISTRY IN THE DOLDRUMS

Delicate cosmetic dentistry is confined to behind the scenes in this film: the on-screen reality is played out in a rather more brutal fashion, with assistant surgeon Higgins extracting one of Slade's teeth with his hands. As Richard McCabe (Higgins) relates, 'Higgins has been taken on board by Maturin primarily because of his expertise in pulling teeth. He's something of a showman – and a charlatan – when it comes to pulling teeth. He's got this black market operation going on whereby he deals in whatever currency's going around on ship: alcohol, laudanum, any kind of drugs. As we witness in the film, he's very susceptible to alcohol…' That's why he pretended to extract a worm – a 'doldrums worm' – together with the tooth: he thought he'd get paid more. Instead, he's shooed away by a resigned, and no doubt regretful, Maturin.

Higgins's activities in O'Brian's novel extend to further excesses of quackery. 'The man was without any sort of doubt an excellent tooth-drawer,' recounts O'Brian in *The Far Side of the World*, 'but he was deeply

ignorant of physic and surgery… furthermore he was beginning to extract illicit fees (as well as eels, mice and earwigs) from those who were sick…'

In the movie, Higgins is clearly out of his depth in different ways. 'I think,' says Richard McCabe, 'that he got into sailing because it's a secure job. It was a steady wage on board ship and three meals a day. And I think it's more to do with that; I don't think he has the constitution of a sailor at all.' He's neither a seaman nor a surgeon, but his presence provides comic vignettes in a film that embraces all human emotions. It also begs the more serious consideration that not everyone was dragged kicking and screaming into the Royal Navy. True, some people went to great lengths to avoid a life at sea. But others made considerable and sometimes ingenious efforts to get to sea in order to make a living.

*Higgins using the latest technology (his hands) to extract a tooth and, so he tries to claim, a 'doldrums worm' from Slade's mouth.*

Although British actors were imported for this movie, 'British' teeth were not. Dentistry of the period was rudimentary in the extreme (false teeth were still made of wood so, theoretically, they could have been in abundant supply). Most of the 'background' cast's teeth were hand-painted with stains, but the principal actors, whose characters gave close-ups, sported '1805' teeth. This was achieved through a technique of 'vacuforming' thin plastic veneers onto the actors' own teeth. Modern dentists use a similar technique for bleaching, but these veneers were painted on the inside in various shades of murkiness and nastiness. In extreme cases, false teeth were incorporated on the veneer. Just look at Awkward Davies. Patrick Gallagher who plays him, has, according to Jim Tyson, 'the nicest teeth in the bunch'. Not in the movie he doesn't.

*Awkward Davies and his equally awkward teeth – veneers added to Patrick Gallagher's real (and splendidly straight) teeth.*

# CHAPTER FOUR

# Jack Aubrey's Navy

## AN AUTHENTIC RECREATION

Seamen have long been regarded as a breed apart; objects of curiosity living in an enclosed world on the fringes of society. The ancient Greeks took rather an extreme view of seafarers and debated whether to count them amongst the living or the dead. In eighteenth century England, they were popularly regarded as very much alive and, literally, kicking: drunken brawling eccentrics who, on land, were like fish out of water. Those preconceptions transferred to print, and paintings of the era depicted sailors ashore dressed in gaudy 'land' rig and rarely in working clothes. That's probably because very little was known about sailors' work. And what *was* known often perpetrated their image as a highly peculiar bunch.

'Nor could I think what world I was in, whether among spirits or devils,' wrote the eponymous author of *Ramblin' Jack: The Journal of Captain John Cremer, 1770–1774*. 'All seemed strange, different language and strange expressions of tongue, that I thought myself always asleep or in a dream, and never properly awake.'

*The popular image of seamen was of miserable, drunken wretches who caused mayhem when on land. Here's an example from caricaturist Thomas Rowlandson,* Portsmouth Point, *painted in 1811.*

*A figure of authority but not a bully. Jack Aubrey was 'not a flogging captain' and treated his men with a respect they reciprocated. The* Surprise *was, by and large, a happy ship.*

History documents many changes in the Navy before the period of the Great Wars with revolutionary and Napoleonic France, from 1793–1815, but the popular stereotype of the drunken sailor remained, and general ignorance of the daily rhythm of life at sea prevails to this day. But the idea that life at sea equated hell on water is, basically, a sweeping and inaccurate generalisation. The life of a seaman in 1805 seems gruesome from a twenty-first century viewpoint, but as historical consultant Gordon Laco puts it, 'even being a pressed seaman was nothing like it was to be poor in Bristol or New York. They were fed plentifully with plain food and there were laws in Parliament controlling the severity of the punishments they could get. It wasn't an easy life by our standards, but on a happy ship it was a good life.' The *Surprise* was, by and large, a happy ship – and believably so. Distinguished naval historian N.A.M. Rodger wrote in the essay 'The Naval World of Jack Aubrey' that 'In default of documentary evidence, scholars must draw on the same materials as the novelist, and there are few who can do so with the imaginative power of Patrick O'Brian'.

The lack of documentary evidence extends to the practicalities of how individual ships were run. There was no Admiralty template: a ship was run according to the captain's personal standing orders. Jack Aubrey's vision of a 'crack ship', as O'Brian recounts in *The Far Side of the World*, 'was one with a strong, highly-skilled crew

*There was very little documentary evidence relating on shipboard life of the era. Most portrayals were stylised, as in* The Quarter-Deck Before Battle *(1818), by John Mitford.*

that could outmanoeuvre and then outshoot the opponent, a taut but happy ship, an efficient man-of-war…' That tautness, happiness and efficiency was instilled by Jack himself, and most of the men who contributed to it had been with him for years. The system, the methodology of the *Surprise*, had been in place for years.

That is axiomatic in this movie: the viewer is plunged in the midst of events, and 'showing' rather than 'telling' applies to the working dynamic of the ship and the comportment of the actors. Nearly all of them are portraying characters so familiar with the *Surprise* that handling her in any situation is almost second nature. Visual effects and technological wizardry have no place here: the only way to show actors recreating a vanished way of life is to have them live that life; and, perforce, to learn it. So, from 'different language and strange expressions of tongue' to the plentiful plain food they ate, the punishments they could get and the weapons they had to fight with, they were required to learn all the ropes.

## Boot Camp

Immediately prior to filming, all actors and extras went through two-weeks' boot camp training which, according to some accounts, was exactly like being back at school. Charts, handouts and reams of research were distributed to everyone – including heads of filming departments. There was written material to read: essays and books by naval scholars including N.A.M. Rodger and Brian Lavery, intricate line-drawings of ships and sails and, for every cast and crew member, a collection of writings thicker than this book on various topics from 'Setting and Dousing the Courses' to 'Small Boat Seamanship' and 'Speaking "Sailor"' as well as a Crew Roster for the *Surprise* and a glossary of sailing terms. Then, to while away the long, lonely hours between evening wrap at around 8pm and call at 6am, a list of titles was supplied for further reading.

Of 'sailor-speak', Sailing Master Andy Reay-Ellers points out that 'for some reason in history, we all speak this sort of fractured, slurred Cockney. If you want to raise the sail, you use the halyard – that's something that derived from haul and yard and it just got slurred into halyard.'

But the majority of the boot camp training was physical: learning to climb the rigging, to row and to fight. Much of the training was actually done out on the *Rose* at sea, in

*This movie was as much about doing as acting. Part of the boot camp training for the actors – the most arduous part – was learning to climb the rigging, usually barefoot, as if it were second nature. After five months, it was second nature.*

# HIERARCHY, MIDSHIPMEN AND MONKEYS

Naval hierarchy was largely a microcosm of British social life, with everyone knowing their 'place' in shipboard society. In the broadest possible terms, there were four major hierarchies within a ship's company: officers, ratings, marines and servants. Yet within those categories were a myriad other distinctions. Some of them ill-defined, others revealing a curious and crucial difference between the Navy and society at large: in the former, people could rise through the ranks; a child from the humblest of backgrounds could rise to become an admiral.

It's the position of a midshipman that illustrates the curious amalgam of official rank and social reality. Midshipmen occupied a limbo between the rank of officers and ratings: officially they were the latter; inferior to warrant officers such as the carpenter, sail-maker or cook. Yet in reality they were officers-in-waiting and were being groomed as such.

Midshipmen were often, but not always, young gentlemen. As of 1794 they were classed by the Admiralty as 'young gentlemen intended

*In the movie, emphasis is placed on the fact that there were children on these ships. They worked — for carpenters and sailmakers and other of the ship's craftsmen — but they also do what all children do: play. Here they're about to stage a mock battle.*

*Some of the smallest children (like Chase, aged ten) were employed as powder monkeys during battle.*

for sea service' but, somewhat perversely, the Admiralty had nothing to do with their appointment; they were chosen by the captain of the ship. Often, like Blakeney, Williamson and Calamy, they would be the teenage sons of friends of the captain. Boyle, the fourth midshipman in the film is, in keeping with the naval 'norm', also a teenager, but the fifth, Hollom is not. On the cusp of thirty, he's regarded as too old to be a midshipman. For the ambitious midshipman, it was desirable to sit the examination for lieutenant as young as possible. Officially midshipmen had to be at least nineteen and have already spent six years at sea in order to sit the examination. Some, however, remained midshipmen throughout most of their naval careers. During the Great Wars there was one, Billy Culmer, who was still a midshipman at the age of fifty-seven.

In the film, the interplay between the midshipmen and their relationships with the rest of the crew provide some of the most acute insights into life at sea, from superstition to death, and

from insubordination to advancement. And, again, they are extremely young: Lord Blakeney, who loses an arm, is only thirteen. In the words of Richard Pates (Williamson), 'I think that's one of the points of this film; to show that it wasn't all fun and games for children in those days. There were children who had to do some quite hectic things on those ships. Go into battle, for instance. Actually kill people.'

And there were other, even younger, children on board, often engaged in the same activities as their land-bound counterparts – playing. 'We were always together,' recalled an author in 1789 who, as a boy, was actually a slave owned by a sea officer, 'and a great part of our time was spent in play.' This, too, is seen in the film, with children staging mock battles, goat races and playing tag. That they are also seen during battle in their incarnation as 'powder monkeys', running hell-for-leather into the bowels of the ship, scooping up gunpowder cartridges and bringing them to the gun crews is a graphic illustration of the flip-side of their lives at sea. So it wasn't all fun and games, but it was part of life within a confined society. Children on ships were often orphans and, at sea, they were looked after, clothed, fed and had somewhere to sleep. There were no such guarantees on land.

*At the boot camp, the cast had to become adept at climbing into the shrouds (left). And they became highly familiar with the origin of the expression 'learning the ropes' (right)...*

order to make it as authentic as possible. Life, as it were, on the ocean wave. Andy Reay-Ellers explains that it was crucial for everyone to know what to do with buntlines, reeflines, clewlines, how to drop a coil and how, basically, not to stand around looking bemused when orders were given.

'It was really important getting them out to sea on the *Rose* so that they could actually get a feel for setting and striking the sails. It gave everyone this sort of casual confidence, which we need to see on screen, because the background actors and the cast themselves are playing people who were virtually born aboard this ship. The actors needed to be almost bored with complex manoeuvres – they needed that level of familiarity.'

Furthermore, the cast needed to feel happy aloft, to jump into the shrouds and run up the ratlines (or 'rattlins' as everyone learned to pronounce them) with the

*Getting the actors out to sea, on the* Rose*, was vital for learning about seamanship.*

same level of confidence. 'We couldn't have people just creeping up the ratlines. They had to be able to run up very quickly.' And this isn't straightforward climbing: there's a point going up the futtock shrouds where you're basically going backwards, leaning over the ship, climbing to a point that you can't actually see. It's nerve-racking and not for the faint-hearted.

The actors can vouch that none of the climbing was done on a pretend basis. Some of them did it barefoot. William Mannering (Faster Doudle) recalls that 'these were tough, hard people: a lot of them went barefoot a lot of the time and the ropes chaff on your feet and your hands. So it's hard: but if I'm asked to climb the mast I've got to look proficient. If I hesitate, it's not truthful.'

Ed Woodall (Mowett) makes the point that most of the training wasn't for the benefit of the camera but for the actors and the ambience itself. 'It's nice to have the confidence to be able to go over to those lines and say "I know what that does…" not that you're necessarily going to need to know that to act the part, but just to be part of the credible world of people at sea. I didn't understand wind. I thought that the obvious thing was if a ship's going to go forward, the wind should be coming from behind it. Not true. The wind has to come from the side, or on the quarter as we seamen say…'

And as for being out on the *Rose* itself, Billy Boyd (Barrett Bonden) recalls that 'when you're not actually working, there's real mellowness to being on a ship with

*A barefoot Nagle, slung in a bosun's chair, repairing the figurehead of the* Surprise.

*Setting sail on the tank. The ship doesn't move, but the wind still blows and the sails have to be set for the camera.*

*The creaking noises on board and eerie sounds from the sea were grist to the mill of the superstitious. Here crew are spooked by the latter as they wait stranded in the doldrums.*

the creaking of the wood, and sometimes dolphins would come up and play in the wake. It's really easy to see how people would get obsessed by it.' Conversely, and as played out in the movie, it's easy to see how suspicion and superstition became integral parts of life at sea. There is nowhere to go – unless you jump overboard. And many, if not most sailors, couldn't swim.

*Rigging the decoy raft on deck.*

Climbing was, by common accord, the most arduous of the boot camp disciplines. (In the Royal Navy of the late eighteenth and early nineteenth century, the word 'discipline' was used in the context of 'training' rather than carrying today's connotation of punishment.) Some actors who had resolved to keep fit by going to the gym soon gave up that idea: climbing rigging was far more strenuous. But the boot camp also involved jolly-boat rowing, small arms training, sword fighting and cannon training. And individual arts were instilled as well: officers' training extended to how to write with a quill pen. Intriguingly, Patrick O'Brian, who wrote longhand, 'very much regretted' that he couldn't write with goose quills.

Given that the smooth running of the *Surprise* was the responsibility of Jack Aubrey and that verisimilitude was the byword of the boot camp, Russell Crowe, as Jack Aubrey, had to assume a certain amount of responsibility here. To a degree that meant being simultaneously authoritarian and a novice during behind-the-scenes training. Crowe explains of being in command: 'to some extent you have to be, but at the same time you're just another bloke having the same experiences as they're having.'

The context of the movie, however, carries inherent advantages here. 'It's about the Navy; rules and regulations. You can see the difference between a midshipman and able seaman, you certainly know the difference between a seaman and a Marine – and you can see at a

glance the difference between a midshipman and an officer.' With this in mind, Crowe had the idea to mirror that hierarchy in the boot camp with different coloured shirts to represent rank: officers in navy blue, midshipmen in light blue, marines in red and the ship's company in white. Carrying this one step further, a T-shirt and sweatshirt represented their 'slops' and long-sleeved shirts their dress uniform. Finally, on the night before boot camp began, every single member of the cast had to sew name badges onto their shirts. 'And,' says Crowe, 'the wardrobe were under strict instructions not to give anyone any help.' A few way-ward souls did ask for help, but they were reported and, finishes Crowe, 'I tackled 'em the next day…'

ABOVE *Midshipmen writing letters home. Calligraphy with a quill was part of the boot camp training.*
BELOW *Hierarchy rules. Only officers and midshipmen had the right to walk the quarterdeck at leisure. Seamen used the forecastle.*

*Boot camp training was vital for learning about the day-to-day running of the ship: about what seamen really did, even in the most adverse conditions.*

Without the context of the film, that may sound gratuitously bossy, but, vitally, there *isn't* a context outside the film. As Crowe puts it, 'People were at their giddiest, you know. It's all fresh and new, there's a mounting wave of enthusiasm so you use that for people to do their tasks. Not,' he adds, 'for them to go to a nightclub in Tijuana. It's good psychology, and the crew have far more interesting things to say about a night spent sewing their names to this film than a night on the tiles.'

The idea of establishing hierarchy from the outset was still reaping rewards even when filming was well underway. As Ian Mercer (Hollar) said, months down the line, 'the job of the bosun is to see to the day-to-day running of the ship and, in instances like being becalmed in the doldrums, it was much more difficult to keep them motivated. You can only do so through discipline,' he continues, 'and as regards that, the T-shirts were a really good idea. Part of the reason why these men were knitted together as a group is the existence of the hierarchy; that, the chain of command, has to exist for it all to work.'

Chris Larkin, (Captain Howard of the Marines), admits to having seen red at boot camp as well as wearing the colour. 'I really *did* shout at these guys,' he recalls. 'Every day. And if they were five minutes late they got a rocket and they had to stand to attention and I'd leave them for twenty minutes. I've yelled at them, screamed at them and had them sewing on badges and so on, and been really kind of fairly unpleasant... The dedication of the extras really surprised me: I've worked with professional extras before and they can be somewhat cynical and world-weary, but my marines are fantastic. When it comes to filming, the more you instil that kind of discipline, the more they got into it. They really worked incredibly hard. I think that'll show in the film... We sat out there in the sun with all the gun belts and muskets and had inspections every day. Everyone else,' he finishes somewhat ruefully, 'had a fairly pleasant time on the boot camp...'

Actually, they didn't – or at least not all the time. It's interesting to hear that some actors really didn't enjoy some aspects of it. It's also probably appropriate that they didn't. The purpose of boot camp training, after all, was to immerse them in as many aspects as possible of life at sea in 1805. It would be pretty unrealistic to expect everybody to relish every moment of that life.

Most people found cannon training had a unique appeal, and Martin Bibbings drilled them in exactly the manner of the era, right down to timing them. Intriguingly, Assistant Directors – the First, Second and Third Lieutenants of the film crew – were trained as well, on the grounds that if they were giving instructions to prepare for filming they had to know what they were filming. For James D'Arcy (Pullings), that training was vital because 'my character is in charge of cannons. So for me the training was one of those times when you wish you could turn yourself into a sponge. You wanted to absorb everything immediately. But, as with most things in life, you just don't get it first time, you have to go back and do it again and again.' And they did: boot camp was the short, sharp treatment, but training in all areas continued all the way through filming.

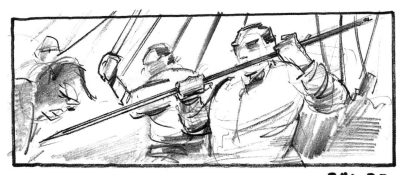

346.20

346.30

*Three of the hundreds of storyboards (these show action on the weather deck of the* Acheron) *drawn to illustrate every aspect of the final battle scene.*

# RATIONS

O'Brian's novels are liberally and sometimes lavishly peppered with scenes of officers and men victualling and carousing. O'Brian himself was something of a gourmand (London's Ritz hotel was a favourite haunt), revelling in the pleasures of fine wine and good food, and his knowledge of officers' and seamen's food in the days of Nelson was so extensive that it spawned a cookbook – *Lobscouse and Spotted Dog – A Gastronomic Companion to the Novels of Patrick O'Brian*. It features – as does this movie – the famous Galapagos Pudding.

The movie also features vignettes of the crew revelling in exotic foods in Brazil, being deprived of water in the doldrums, bemoaning diet of penguin in the Great South Sea, and, in the case of Nagle's insubordination, of drunkenness (note that Jack uses the expression 'three sheets to the wind'). In short, the film gives an accurate portrayal of both the best and the worst of eating and drinking at sea.

As O'Brian writes in *The Far Side of The World*, 'Even a sixth-rate man-of-war needed an astonishing amount in the way of naval stores, while each of the warriors she carried was allowed seven pounds of biscuits a week, seven gallons of beer, four pounds of beef and two of pork, a quart of peas, a pint and a half of oatmeal, six ounces of sugar and the same of butter, twelve ounces of cheese and half a pint of vinegar, to say nothing of the lime juice, the necessary enormous quantity of fresh water for steeping the salt meat...'

For the ordinary seaman, that basically distilled down to a breakfast of burgoo (a mixture of oatmeal and water) or 'scotch coffee' (burned bread boiled in water and sweetened with sugar) and dinner of weevily biscuits, sauerkraut and salted meat ('stony, fibrous, shrunken, dark and gristly' according to one account). It sounds perfectly foul to us, but it was often superior to anything they might get on land. More importantly – and except in the most adverse circumstances – there was a guaranteed, regular supply of food on board ship. Officers, however, usually had the means to supply their own food in the shape of their own livestock. Their meat couldn't have been fresher: cattle, sheep, pigs, goats, hens and geese

*Fresh fruit and urgent supplies being carried on-board from the Brazilian coast.*

would have been running around on deck only hours before they were eaten. Some animals were kept as pets. In the movie, Aspasia the goat (named after an ancient Greek of great intellect and beauty) is half pet and half provider of milk.

As for alcohol, the ration of a gallon of beer a day indicates that, for those with a will, there was always a way to get more. Even for a relatively small ship of 197 souls, there was a vast amount of strong beer on board. Strong, as opposed to 'small' beer was issued for long voyages – the greater alcoholic content meant it had a longer shelf life. For ships assigned to the Mediterranean, wine was issued and, following the capture of Jamaica by the British in 1665, rum was the (wildly popular) addition, in the form of grog.

Officers, again, were a breed apart. Especially captains. In one of O'Brian's books, Jack relates to Stephen how he's known captains to go mad, become tyrants or, most commonly, take to drink. Some captains drank themselves to death, recording in their journals the impossible burden of responsibility and the extreme isolation of their position. One of the principal reasons why the O'Brian books work so joyously is, to put it at its simplest, that Jack has Stephen to play with. Yes, they play the violin and cello together, but that accompaniment is symbolic of something deeper as well; of friendship at its purest and most platonic.

There are only oblique references to drunkenness in this movie: Calamy, looking flushed and slightly the worse for wear during dinner (well, he is only 13...) and Nagle being drunk when he insults Hollom. There is, too, a fleeting nod to another method of getting loaded – Stephen taking laudanum (in the books, he's an addict) after an argument with Jack. But, as with every aspect of life in Nelson's Navy, the reality of drunkenness was thoroughly researched. There *was* incredible drinking in the Navy, and the armed forces are still renowned for their ability to imbibe astonishing quantities. Yet then, as now, decorum was paramount. It was perfectly acceptable for officers to fall down drunk – as long as they didn't disgrace themselves prior to becoming insensible. As Peter Weir says, 'it was fine to hold it to the point of falling over: many a naval officer who'd gone to another ship for a drink would be lowered off the side in a sort of bosun's chair and rowed home insensible. That was okay. But you didn't slur your words and you didn't lose your proper naval manner...' You didn't, basically, lose your British stiff upper lip.

Of things British, the term 'limey' was, as is well known, coined by American seamen after the Royal Navy adopted the practise of using lime (or lemon) juice as both prevention against and cure for what, until then, had been the biggest killer at sea – scurvy. The antiscorbutic properties of those fruits against the dreaded disease was published by one Dr James Lund in 1753, and the practice of using the juice became regulation in the Navy in 1795. Lemons were actually more effective then limes: O'Brian probably knew this, writing in *The Wine Dark Sea* that 'Stephen could oblige the seamen to avoid scurvy by drinking lemon juice in their grog'. Yet limes, not lemons, are usually credited with winning the battle against scurvy: the word 'limey' persisted and passed into common parlance, although 'limejuicers' – British ships – has not survived.

*Cannon training
reaping its rewards:
in the thick of battle
on the gun deck.*

The particular difficulty of cannon training was the confined space of the gun deck. 'It's a wonderful bit of teamwork,' recalls George Innes (Joe Plaice). 'And they were timing us to come in under a certain time. It's incredible really, but we did it – and we didn't bang our heads. People do, you know. There's not enough headroom. There are people wandering around with head injuries – and they're not from trepanning…'

'It's always exciting for an actor,' says Alex Palmer (Slade), 'to be trained to do something you're never ever going to do. We're never, ever going to fire cannons, but we get to have a little taste of what it might have been like. And everyone seemed to take pride in getting up to speed. There was quite a bit of competition going on between cannon crews. I might add that my cannon crew is obviously the fastest …'

Ed Woodall (Mowett) makes a salient point reflecting back to the issue of authenticity. 'I found looking at some of the other, older films that cannons recoil and then fall over on top of somebody. Then they pull the cannons back to get them out. You just can't, *clearly* you can't do that. They're so heavy. They're huge, these cannons. Obviously they've got to be made lighter for the film, but they're as authentic as was possible.'

Russell Crowe, in between training for all of the above (as well as for a complex series of swordfights and violin lessons every day), had to keep one eye on leadership and motivation. 'Part of this is about setting a certain programme that will keep people inquisitive,' he says. 'Six weeks in, I took all the cast up to San Diego. We stayed in a hotel, had a big dinner and the next day we went to Seaworld where everyone swam with dolphins... you know, things they would have had the opportunity of doing on a real ship. It's not like these are instructions,' he continues, 'but these things are following the thematic of leadership that Peter set: he allows you to be imaginative in your role as the supposed leader. This sort of thing fuels imagination, and if your imagination is fuelled then the characters are fuelled. It all pays off in the end.'

'I don't really fit into the military thing,' says Paul Bettany. 'I didn't have to do the boot camp. They did call me in, but I said "no". I went and learned about dissecting fish instead. It's fascinating in its own smelly way.' This was done for instruction in what Jack disparagingly refers to on one occasion as Stephen's 'hobbies'. For his role as the doctor, Bettany needed to acquire a few additional skills. Prior to filming, he went with Peter Weir to see a surgeon in London who is also a historian at the Royal College of Surgeons. 'It's one of the edifying things about being an actor... you get to immerse yourselves in other people's lives.' And in their bodies. 'The *Surprise*'s crew,' wrote Patrick O'Brian, 'like most seamen, were a hypochondriacal set of ghouls upon the whole, and they loved a surgical operation almost as much as they loved a prize.' O'Brian goes on to describe a trepanning operation, one that 'Dr Maturin had carried out at sea before... and many of them had seen him do so.'

*Paul Bettany was spared the boot camp to take instruction in amputation. Here are the fruits of his researches: Lord Blakeney (Max Pirkis) surrounded by his fellow midshipmen after Stephen Maturin's removal of his injured right arm.*

*'Physician he is,' says seaman Slade of Stephen Maturin. 'Not one of your common surgeons.' Note the fashionable forward-brushed 'Napoleon' haircut.*

Apart from ghoulishness, the main reason why so many of the crew witnessed Stephen's operations was that he needed light, and therefore the open air, to perform them. Fleets had hospital ships accompanying them but, for lone voyagers like the *Surprise*, the official ship's 'hospitals' of the day were the surgeon's cockpits, grim little holes where operations would be performed with the aid of rum, a leather gag, candlelight and boiling pitch to cauterise amputated limbs.

The *Surprise* is in fact fortunate to have Stephen Maturin on board. He is a physician, the highest order of doctor at the time, and it was highly unusual for someone in that position to be a ship's surgeon. Interestingly – especially for a Catholic – his skills would necessitate experience in human dissection. At the time, and until the Anatomy Act of 1832, dissection deprived a body of a grave and was therefore a fate infinitely worse than death. The bodies used by medical students were invariably provided by body-snatchers...

But back to trepanning. Maturin performs the operation on the *Surprise* in his professionally dispassionate manner. Correspondingly, Paul Bettany describes it as 'actually quite easy' but, also entirely aptly, Richard McCabe as his grossly ineffectual assistant Higgins, was horrified by it. 'The make-up department did quite

*A bad hair day: the trepanning operation on Joe Plaice's skull. From the script: 'Stephen's drill carves out a neat disc of bone to reveal a purplish mass which he starts spooning from the cavity...'*

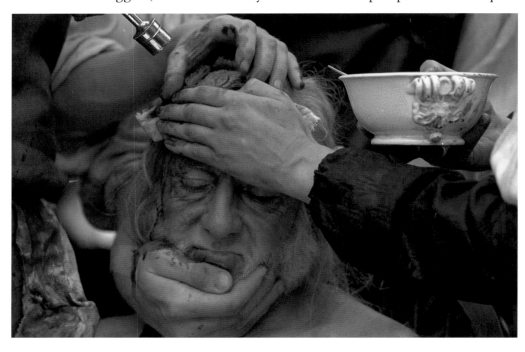

*Maturin is helped – or rather hindered – at the sickbed by his questionably qualified assistant Higgins (Richard McCabe).*

the most extraordinary job on his [Joe Plaice's] head… all the skin on his head had been peeled back like an orange and there was a little circular area of skull that we took out to reveal the brain underneath… it was absolutely revolting.'

McCabe was also privileged to observe the other operations. 'Blakeney's arm… oh it's disgusting. I'm watching the sawing off of an arm… oh my God.' McCabe looks sick, shudders and then laughs. 'Well, that's my character through and through, I think.'

And on Stephen's operation on himself: 'It's blind terror followed by revulsion when you see that injury. I had nightmares, you know, after filming. We were doing the operation and nobody had warned us about the blood that was being pumped up through the wound. So when Maturin cut into himself, it was just so authentic. The reactions of all the actors who were around were genuine ones. It was quite, quite horrendous and gave you an insight into how operations of that time would have been dealt with,' he finishes with a grimace. 'You really need a strong stomach. Looking at it and mopping it all up was really nauseating…'

*Stephen recuperating from his stomach operation he performed on himself. His protégé Blakeney (Max Pirkis) and his servant Padeen (John De Santis) show him the fruits of their explorations on the Galapagos Islands.*

# SWORD FIGHTING

'We collect rare texts on sword fighting. We actually have original texts – and I don't mean copies – going back to 1568. And we have actual texts of the way people were trained in the Napoleonic era for the use of the cutlass, as well as for a variety of other weapons.'

Dan Speaker and his wife Jan Bryant are the sword masters on this film. Bryant, in fact, is the only professional female sword master in the film industry. Speaker has been captivated by theatrical sword fighting since he was six, and trained at the Royal Scottish Academy of Music and Drama. Bryant initially trained and worked as a dancer, and therein lies the key to the unique combination of talents: the direct correlation between dance and sword fighting. 'Especially,' adds Bryant, 'at the

classical small sword period around the time of Louis XIV. He hired people to codify the teaching methodology.' A methodology, it transpires, that had started to develop in the mid-sixteenth century when sword fighting evolved from the hack and slash of medieval times into a more scientific art.

But, for this movie, we're in 1805 when guns and cannonry were the predominant fighting instruments. Sword fighting had reverted to a more hack-and-slash method, although not, by and large, when it came to the officers. 'By that time,' explains Speaker, 'the British military had learned a lot from the French, particularly from a guy who had come over in the 1700s and started a school, the House of Angelo, where a lot of the British officers were taught.'

'So officers would be far more highly skilled than your average sailors in the period in which this movie is set,' continues Bryant, 'and therefore have a very different look to them. Sailors and idlers are primarily involved with making the ship work, but in a fight… well, they have to fight. And they would have a knife-style of sword – basically a cutlass, which is not in fact a sword but a long knife.' (One theory has it that cutlasses were actually modelled on sailors' rigging knives.)

So the aim for the movie was not to teach musketeers to fight with elegant rapiers, but instead a

*Russell Crowe despatching one of the twenty or so Frenchmen he faces during the final battle. By 1805, swords had been largely replaced by guns and cannonry as the predominant fighting instruments, but officers (and Russell Crowe) still received formal training in swordplay.*

*In the thick of the final battle. Close-range combat was minutely choreographed and, whilst officers used swords as well as guns, seamen used cutlasses (actually a type of knife) or anything that came to hand. Including (far left) their hands...*

range of characters with backgrounds ranging from the sophisticated to the brutal, and they all had to be trained by Speaker and Bryant. 'Even though it's not going to be beautiful footwork that you'll see on film, that's where we start off,' says Bryant. 'The footwork's where it starts, and these guys have to know how to balance themselves so they can believe they're actually fighting. A lot of them haven't ever been in a knife fight and it doesn't come naturally – so it has to be taught.'

A range of different factors have to be taken into account, physical mannerisms for a start. If you're an officer, and particularly a nobleman, of the time you'll have a completely different carriage to an ordinary seaman who spends his day climbing and repairing rigging. And, adds Bryant, 'If your character owns land, has horses, wears

riding boots – all those things come into it and we need to get them sorted out from the beginning. Physical mannerisms are really important.' She adds that 'We've had guys coming in here playing officers and they didn't have the carriage *at all*. Now I'm really proud of them. I look at them and go "I believe that".'

The methodology Speaker and Bryant have used has been refined over years of working in film and theatre. Coupling swordplay with ideas modified from dance training, they also have to incorporate a particularly vital element – safety. 'We can't have people poking each other's eyes out or whacking each other on the nose,' says Speaker. 'And believe me, it's really easy to do.'

And they make their job sound pretty easy as well. 'The training is ongoing, but at the boot camp we did the twenty-five principal cast and the 120 or so they're calling extras. But they're not really extras because they're the crew of the *Surprise*. We trained in groups of 20–30. We can train groups of 100 if we have enough space and volume.'

Ed Woodall bears the fruits of their lessons. 'For me sword fighting was a really new thing, I *so* enjoyed getting that together. I've got this great big curvy sword... I didn't know this at the beginning but it's developed this fantastic slicing sort of fighting style.' Then he looks up, eyes glinting. 'Mowett's a poet, you know, he's a sensitive man. But when it gets to the final battle, this guy is a butcher...'

## Prizes and Privateers

'They are already counting their share of the prize money,' announces Jack to Stephen as they head for the Galapagos in pursuit of the *Acheron*. Jack's motives are more complex than just money but, for the crew, the prize of the French ship means rich pickings indeed. By capturing an enemy battleship or privateer and sailing it back to an English or neutral port, the victorious crew stood to make money – sometimes a great deal of it.

The possibility of prizes was a huge incentive to join the Navy. The sales pitch for the Royal Marines made no bones about it: a recruitment poster of the period, rather than promoting the job itself, plugs the free food on board ship and the possibility of untold riches. 'What man of spirit,' it finishes, 'would fail to seize such an opportunity?'

In reality, earning a great deal from prizes was the exception rather than the rule, but the staggering amounts of money to be made, combined with the meritocracy of naval advancement, lent enormous appeal to the service. Most of the value of a ship and its cargo would be shared by the captain and crew, the former receiving the lion's share. The Crown also received a share, a process that was formalised during the reign of Henry VIII.

A captain at the beginning of the nineteenth century could net the equivalent of thirty-five years' pay from one prize, and there are numerous records of vast estates being purchased with the spoils. So attractive were the possibilities on offer that captains and even admirals were not averse to nipping off from their fleets and doing a bit of privateering on the sly. Yet even an ordinary seaman may have earned

*Calamy (Max Benitz) eyeing the privateer* Acheron – *later to become the prize shared by all on board the* Surprise.

£10 from a good prize – not bad compared to a wage of 24 shillings a month. Again, this concept of earning extra money – far in excess of anything ordinary men could earn on land – flies in the face of the image of a gruesome and penurious life at sea.

Russell Crowe explains of the prizes in Aubrey's time: 'Even though the Navy and prize money became more formalised under Henry VIII, sailors are still benefiting from their piratical beginnings, and Jack's pretty focussed on what prizes meant to them – and also what they meant to him when he's back on land.' The sobriquet 'Lucky Jack' doesn't just apply to his seamanship – it's also a nod to its potential rewards for all and sundry.

The downside, however, is that the primary function of a warship like the *Surprise* is to destroy the enemy – even at the cost of its own destruction. Here is the key to the difference between the *Surprise* and the privateer *Acheron*: the role of the latter, first and foremost, is to make money and then go home. That is its weakness – and Jack Aubrey knows it. Even having a small warship like the *Surprise* dogging its heels is a huge problem.

The *Acheron* may be shrouded in mystery, but her role is quite clear: she is disrupting the enormously lucrative British whaling trade. As mentioned in Chapter Two, there's a historical precedent here: the USS *Essex*, on which O'Brian based the *Norfolk* in *The Far Side of the World*, was doing just that. But the *Essex* was American and the year was 1812. Here, we're in 1805 and the *Acheron* is French, which raises some intriguing questions about both history and this movie – and indeed the confluence of the two.

Gordon Laco has some pretty intriguing theories about the *Acheron* – and some hard facts. He previously worked on a documentary about the *Essex* whaling ship disaster and knows the subject well. 'After their revolution (the War of Independence), the US were furiously trying to build themselves a Navy, but they weren't well funded. And they had war debts to the French which they couldn't pay in cash, so they gave them several ships instead. Also, there were other ships under construction, ordered by the Navy. But the government couldn't pay for them, so rather than face bankruptcy they put the ships up for auction. Several ships were recorded as "sold foreign at auction", so we could assume the *Acheron* is one of those.'

Further speculation, again based on fact, surrounds the owners of the *Acheron*. 'We thought about the possibility of a syndicate of wealthy French ship owners,' says Laco. 'They may well be facing bankruptcy themselves because of the blockade during the war, so they might have decided to club together to go privateering as a source of revenue. They could have pooled resources to buy a frigate and ship it back from the States.' That's akin to today's businessmen grouping together to buy an aircraft carrier to ship arms: the potential rewards were so great that such an enterprise would make economic sense. The difference is the cargo: the *Acheron* was after whale oil. And, in 1805, that oil was incredibly valuable.

Which brings us straight back to the movie, and to the fact that, in the Galapagos, the *Acheron* has robbed the British whalers of £100,000 worth of whale oil – the fruits of two solid years of whaling. Add the possibility of spermaceti (the most valuable of whale oils) and ambergris, the solid by-product of whale oil mentioned by Mowett in his pre-battle poem, and the on-screen action dovetails with the historical backdrop of both prizes and privateers – and the question of money. Little of this is mentioned in the script, but all of it was researched.

With his experience on the *Essex* documentary, Gordon Laco was familiar with the economics of whale oil, ambergris and spermaceti (found in a cavity in a whale's head – hence the name sperm whale). Then, as now, oil was a tradable commodity and, in 1805, was worth £32 per ton at the wharf in England. A small ship of 350 tons' burden – as Hogg's was calculated to be – would, at full capacity, be carrying cargo worth £11,200. Add the worth of the spermaceti and the figure increases to £14,000. 'The breakeven point for a voyage,' says Laco, 'was reckoned to be twenty whales. At two tons per whale, that means the expenses of the entire voyage were £1280.' The profit, then, would be a cool £12,750 – and this in an age when a prosperous merchant in Colchester could house and feed his wife, four children and servants for £350 a year. Or, at the other end of the scale, an age when Jane Austen's Mr Darcy was considered to be obscenely rich on an income of £10,000 a year. 'I told Peter,' finishes a wistful Laco, 'that we're in the wrong business.'

So the economics of privateers, prizes, trade and warfare have been minutely examined to fit the 'back story' of the film. Layer upon layer is hidden beneath the canvas on which the *Surprise* overwhelms the mighty *Acheron*. And it's not just for the benefit of the viewer or the O'Brian fan: it was always a prerequisite for the cast to have flesh to add to the bones of the script. 'Other ships,' says one cast member, 'are being recalled... we're on the eve of Trafalgar, remember. But the *Surprise* is an old ship, she may even be on the point of being decommissioned. So she's not needed for the fleet, but she's available to intercept the *Acheron*.'

Even the possible attitude of the French government was taken into account. With maybe two dozen unprotected British whalers in the Pacific, each worth £14,000, the knock-on effect of the loss to the British could be enormous. 'You never know,' muses Gordon Laco. 'With patriotic Frenchmen in the government issuing privateering licences... maybe the government itself would have put money into the *Acheron* trip. It's not a naval ship, but you can see a Napoleonic "N" on her. A privateer wouldn't normally have an imperial symbol... And if the whole whale oil crop was decimated by the *Acheron*, there could well be a stock market crash in London...'

# MUSIC

'It is probably fair to say,' wrote Patrick O'Brian, 'that the sea-officers of that time knew more about music, serious music, than their modern counterparts, above all in the matter of playing themselves, improvising and even composing; for at that period the cult of Philistinism, so general in this century, had not yet invaded the fighting services…'

Peter Weir's passionate interest in music would probably have gratified O'Brian. Music is always an important, integral and often mesmeric element of the director's films, and this one is no exception. (Peter Weir, as mentioned, played all types of music, all the time, on set.) The added bonus is that Russell Crowe and Paul Bettany went

*A soulful Hollom strumming his guitar. Whilst officers played and listened to 'serious' music, the musical legacy of ship-board life is from the ballads of ordinary sailors.*

to enormous lengths to acquire the violin and cello skills of Aubrey and Maturin. They had lessons every day for months: when you see them playing pieces by, for example, Mozart or Boccherini, they really *are* playing them. No hand doubles here.

O'Brian himself didn't play any musical instrument, but his knowledge of the music of the period, and of what officers did or did not know is, as ever, encyclopaedic:

'…it is certain that they attended concerts and the opera, above all in Lisbon and the Mediterranean ports, in remarkably large numbers… for the people I write about, music would for most purposes have come to an end with Mozart, apart from some occasional stragglers like Clementi and Hummel… even so, what vast expanses of joy and delight lie between these limits… and it is in these wide plains, this great wealth of talent that Aubrey and Maturin wandered at large whenever the duty, the dangers of the sea and the violence of the enemy allowed them to do so.'

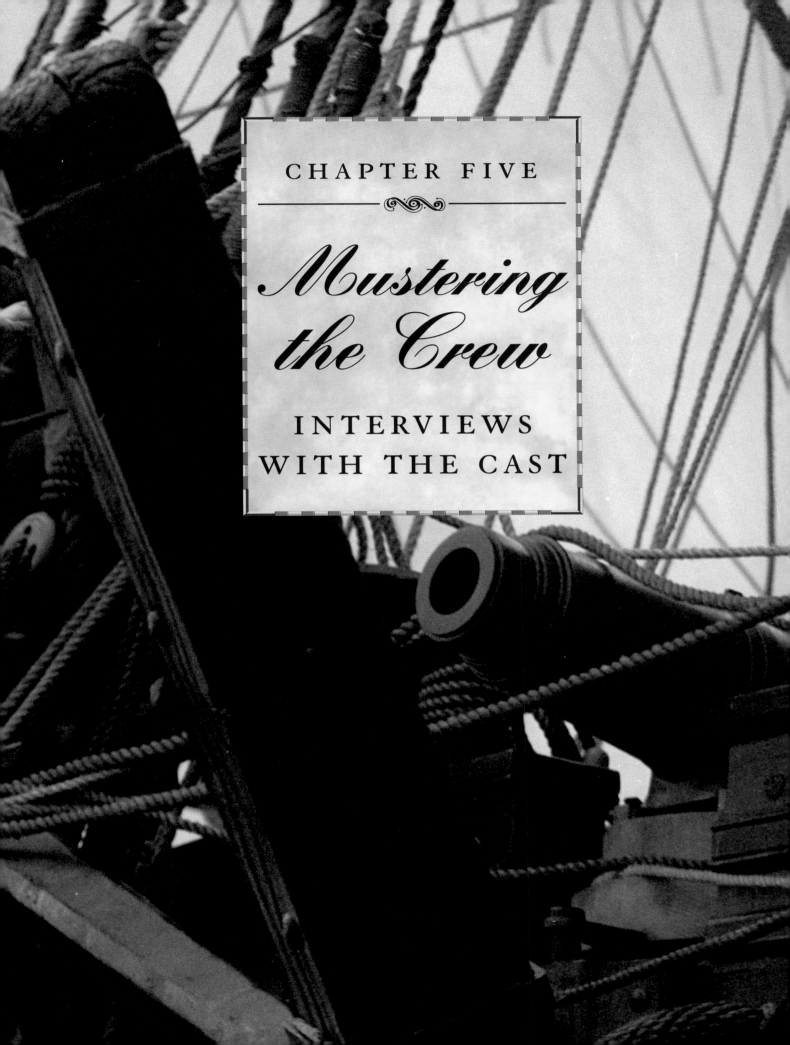

CHAPTER FIVE

# Mustering the Crew

INTERVIEWS
WITH THE CAST

## Russell Crowe

'The view of the world from up there,' says Russell Crowe, 'is its own reward. It's really *quite* special.'

It's also quite scary. 'Up there' is at the top of the main mast of the *Surprise*, some 138 vertiginous feet above the deck. From that distance, the *Surprise* looks like a canapé, not a ship. And, from the deck, anyone aloft looks more like a decoration than a person. It can be dangerous: especially if you're not attached to a safety wire. 'Yes,' chuckles Crowe, 'Tom Rothman [Co-Chairman of Fox] wasn't very pleased about that. He phoned me up to ask me what the hell I was doing…'

Crowe has a very good explanation for why the hell he wasn't wearing a safety line. But his own feelings about climbing the rigging are just as intriguing: 'I didn't like heights. I didn't like the idea of climbing the rigging. But Jack does. So up the rigging you go…'

Patrick O'Brian referred to Jack Aubrey as 'the most resolute of fighting captains', and the same could be said for Russell Crowe. The determination, the physicality, the innate air of authority and the bluff humour are the same. And they share something that works on a visceral level as well. Jack isn't 'just' a ship's captain and Russell Crowe isn't 'just' a Hollywood star. As Chris Larkin puts it: 'I don't think calling him a "classic leading man" does Russell justice, because it just infers good looks and Hollywood things like that. It's not about that. It's about something deeper: it's about what makes someone follow you. Nelson was a skinny little guy, about five foot four with one arm and one eye, and people followed him to the ends of the earth. That's what it's about.'

'He has a natural authority,' says Peter Weir. 'He was born to be a captain: a captain of actors and a captain of a ship. A

*'… people may call Jack a Republican or a Conservative,'* comments Russell Crowe, *'But he is absolutely neither of those. He's far too much of a humanist. He operates on a level of politics we just don't have any more. It's far broader, far more understanding.'*

movie star is a very rare creature – even rarer if they're also a good actor. It's as much as you can ask for.'

Of Jack, Russell Crowe says that 'he *had* to be a patriarch. If you want him to be the man you think he is, then he has to be concerned with the welfare of every person on board. The more effort Jack puts into the teaching of these young men then the easier his life is. There's a very practical side – but there's also a very human side. He doesn't want anyone under his charge to fail themselves or what is required by the community of the ship.'

Crowe adopted that attitude before filming began. During boot camp he was, basically, Jack Aubrey. 'In a way you have to be… in this type of movie you want a certain rhythm and hierarchy established because that's what it's all about.' Yet Crowe gives the greatest credit for that to Peter Weir. 'If you don't have someone like Peter who allows you to be imaginative in your role as the supposed leader then you don't get the opportunity to do these things.'

Crowe nearly didn't seize the opportunity at all. 'I wasn't,' he says frankly, 'turned on by the first script Peter presented me with – but I did want to work with him.' The long development of the script and the organic nature of the shooting script is something that has been much discussed in this book, but Crowe is adamant about his absolute commitment to the source material, 'to becoming an expert on your character from the way O'Brian had his characters talk. It's vital.'

*The burden of responsibility drove some captains to the brink – or to drink. Jack Aubrey's favoured stimulant in the small hours is coffee. A skilled mathematician, here he's charting the course for the action to come.*

It's vital, too, that Jack talks differently to Stephen Maturin than he does to anyone else. 'Stephen,' says Russell Crowe, 'is Jack's saviour in many ways. He's the outlet for the art that works inside this otherwise monolithic figure of authority: he *needs* Stephen to be there. Yes, he's a very talented surgeon and he's going to give Jack and his men a better chance of survival, but he's also outside the sailors' world; he can give Jack simple and objective opinions. They have a very, very different view of the world; they also come to cross words, but at the same time they're both reasonable enough men to realise the size of the planet they travel on and how much they need each other. There are,' he finishes, 'freedoms of expression he allows Stephen that he just cannot allow with his officers.'

Indeed there are. And with his fellow officers, Jack has to employ a modus operandi – almost a mantra – that Russell Crowe adhered to in his interpretation of the character. 'Jack,' he says, 'had to be

"always definite – but not necessarily correct". You have to train your men,' he continues, 'to respond to your being definite and not to question the moment. It's apparent in ocean-racing now. That's the way a boat works.'

It works in another way as well: by setting an example. That's partly what Russell Crowe was doing at the top of the mast without a safety line. 'If I don't take on physical responsibilities that would be second nature to Jack then the response of the actors – and especially the real sailors on this ship – would be less than automatic. Doing things like that, you hope that, incrementally, you can win their trust.'

The other reason for the lack of a safety line was to give Peter Weir one hundred per cent of what he wanted to shoot: a safety line limits a shot. 'That's what I told Tom Rothman,' says Crowe with a grin. 'I said I was giving him the opportunity for a better shot. He said what if I fell off? So I told him, "Mate, you change your priorities when you do it this way. You stick to rule number one: Hold on! It's that simple…"'

*Jack's view of the world is very different to that of Stephen Maturin, yet the relationship between the two men is central to the movie. Although in a position of supreme authority (a ship's captain wielded more power than the King), Jack was well aware, as Russell Crowe says, that he has to be 'always definite – but not necessarily correct.'*

## Paul Bettany

To call Paul Bettany a chameleon would, in a sense, be an insult. 'I hate chameleons,' he says with vehemence. 'I hate bugs: they're alive and they do their own thing and they frighten me. There was one in particular: a great big, shiny blue thing that flies. It flew at me so I screamed and ran off set.'

But Bettany is an actor of startling accomplishment who can, it seems, effortlessly assume the reptilian gaze of the iguanas he loathes – 'they stink' – to play the enigmatic Maturin.

'To my intense delight,' says Peter Weir. 'I watched Paul take the character and make it his own, and yet at the same time have him deeply rooted in O'Brian's writing.'

'Stephen Maturin,' says Bettany, 'is one of those people who, if you put them in solitary confinement for months on end, would come out exactly as they went in. He has so many personal resources, he's so self-contained that he can really live inside himself.' As, indeed, Patrick O'Brian lived within Maturin. 'I was intrigued by O'Brian and the way he conducted himself in interviews. He seemed to be amused from within himself; you could see him chuckling inwardly – it didn't seem to matter whether other people got it or not.'

Paul Bettany clearly 'got it'. He mentions the shared acerbic wit of both O'Brian and Maturin, the interest in naturalism, the quietness and the experience in espionage. As regards the latter 'you don't know any of that stuff in the movie. That doesn't matter, but it's wealth to me. It's just one of those little things that fill the inner life of your character, to make him breathe a little bit more.' For the outer manifestations of his character, Bettany quips that 'it's fabulous having someone more studious and resourceful than you handing you a

*'He's really a product of the Enlightenment,' says Peter Weir of Stephen Maturin. 'He is, if you like, a modern man.' Unlike Jack Aubrey, who the director says is the sort of hero who has 'gone from this world'.*

massive great manila envelope with endless kinds of research in it.' Yet he's being a little disingenuous about the ease of it all: he had to learn a lot – as demonstrated by the facility and sometimes passion with which he talks about medicine, God, natural history, Darwin and, of course, the cello, his accompaniment to Jack's violin.

'It's a really odd relationship because music is the only thing they seem to have in common. I'm completely anti-authority, and it's Jack's bread and butter, regimentation is part of his daily life. They have completely different ways of viewing the world. But, you know, they have the sort of deep relationship that you have with your best friend: you know the insides of him, so when he's in pieces you know how to put him back together again…'

Bettany doesn't apply those sentiments to his cello, part of the glue that binds them together. He would happily see it in pieces. 'Oh it's a *ghastly* instrument. And, no, I won't play you a tune. It sounds like I'm trying to climb into a squirrel.'

*'Stephen Maturin,' says Paul Bettany, 'studies people in the same way he studies animals. He certainly studies Jack, and what he finds intriguing is that Jack is the exception to the rule that absolute power corrupts.'*

## *The Crew of the HMS* Surprise

'It's the Napoleonic Wars and the French are better cooks – so we're chasing them.' **David Threlfall**, playing Jack's wonderfully curmudgeonly steward **Killick** is of course, joking, but there *is* something of his character in the remark. 'Killick is happier not to know why the captain is so determined to pursue the *Acheron*. I think he's less likely to have an opinion about the *Acheron* than he is over where the silver goes and what you do with it.' (In the books, Killick is described as wry, shrewish and hopeless at everything except ironing and polishing silver.) 'In the middle of the action,' continues Threlfall, 'when the ship has a hole in the side, his concern is to save the silver.'

Killick is a fabulous creation. 'He's a bit like the Shakespearean all-licensed fool,' says Threlfall. 'In other words, he's not a fool at all, and he speaks to the

*David Threlfall plays Jack Aubrey's servant Killick. Cantankerous and over-familiar, he is nevertheless the epitome of the supremely loyal servant. And he has a very odd Christian name: Preserved.*

captain as no one else can. If something's not right, he'll say it's not right.' Cantankerous and over-familiar ('no music?' he says to Jack at one point. 'That's a relief') he has also, somehow, assumed a moral ascendancy over Jack. The complex background to that, says Threlfall, is both in the books and in history. 'His character is inspired by Nelson's manservant Tom Allen. I think Aubrey picked Killick up in the same way that Nelson picked up Allen — because of something he did. I've taken that on. I know what he did and I have my own theory about where Aubrey met Killick, but I don't really want to tell people…'

The character of Killick may not have much to do with fighting or with sailing but everything about him — from his domain to his distinctive manner of speaking — was minutely researched. 'Toasted cheese,' says Threlfall, 'I mean, how do you do that in 1805? We researched it. And if there's any doubt, you pull in one of the experts. So from the fighting tops to toasted cheese to what you would say when the food arrives on a table on board a ship in 1805 — it's all there.'

Of himself, the actor says that, 'It wouldn't have suited me *at all* to live on a ship. I love the sea and have a great respect for it… but in another life I would have had to be pressed on board, and then been depressed. I shall walk the gang-plank for saying that…'

'A lot of films,' says **James D'Arcy (First Lieutenant Tom Pullings)**, 'carry the expectation that the audience is stupid. They have to be sledgehammered at the beginning with every piece of information that'll be important at the end. This film isn't like that. It's much more cinema as art form. It has the feel of an independent film — but just happens to have a vast budget.'

It was a budget that enabled D'Arcy to have the 'once in a lifetime experience' of climbing to the top of the *Rose* out on the ocean. 'That was my Hollywood moment,' he grins, 'It was really extraordinary. We [he was with Russell Crowe] were in the middle of the ocean, 150 feet in the air: just the two of us with a helicopter coming in to film us in close up. You're told to keep your eye on the horizon to stop yourself feeling sick, but it was difficult *not* to do that – the sun was setting over the ocean. It was beautiful – one of those moments of absolute exhilaration.'

Although Pullings, in the books, is 'not a gentleman' (referring to his birth rather than his manners) he is, says D'Arcy, 'A really nice guy. And he's really well-respected. Not complicated. You know,' he adds, 'my view is that they weren't complicated men. They didn't have enough time to think about themselves. It's a bit like being here, actually. You're a bit disjointed from your life, which uncomplicates things very quickly. We all have friends, relationships, bank statements and so on to go back to – but not here. It's exactly like going out to sea for six months.'

*James D'Arcy plays First Lieutenant Pullings, one of Jack's most loyal and able followers. He's now second-in-command of the* Surprise; *'a ship,' says D'Arcy after intensive training in seamanship, 'that I could theoretically sail – although I wouldn't like to put it to the test...'*

For which, on a physical level, the boot camp was invaluable preparation – although D'Arcy smiles at the mention of it. 'Everyone keeps referring to this "boot camp" as if it involved us doing press-ups at six in the morning. It was absolutely nothing of the sort – it was two weeks of invaluable training. The research we'd done was one thing: you can read all you like, but until you actually fire cannons and sail these ships none of it makes much sense.'

A concept familiar to **Midshipman Hollom**, played by **Lee Ingleby**. 'He struggles. He just struggles. He's not suited to the sea. And through no fault of his own, he's not liked. I think he'd be happier,' he adds with a laugh, 'being a poet or doing something artistic.' But Hollom is a reluctant midshipman, far older than his peers and, as Jack points out, one who has already failed twice to pass for lieutenant. A conversation with Jack informs us of this – and his uniform suggests it. 'He's growing out of his uniform and he can't afford a new one. He's a man now rather than a boy but he still has his rather old-fashioned uniform. And it's too tight.' Jack is far from unsympathetic but, at the end of the day, he doesn't really understand Hollom. 'Hollom panics and, at the same time, he tries to keep everything harmonious, so he lacks respect from his men. And, of course, the crew thinks he's completely jinxed – the Jonah.' That, ultimately, is the nail in Hollom's coffin: seamen of the time were fantastically supersti-

*Midshipman Hollom. 'He's just not cut out for the sea,' says Lee Ingleby. 'Or for responsibility. He wants people to like him.' Instead they come to despise him and he becomes a jinx on the ship – the dreaded Jonah.*

tious. 'He's a bit like me really, I sort of try to find good in everyone,' explains Ingleby. 'I sympathise with him – I want to be his friend. It's a fantastic character to play; a character going through paranoia, the loneliness, the despair. And, ultimately, to suicide.'

Of the ship, Ingleby says 'When I first saw it, I thought, "Wow, that's going to be our home for the next how-ever many months". And it would have been the same for the sailors – that's their England. Learning about the el-ements of this floating city is fascinat-ing; reading about floggings, crimes, people's duties. You really wanted to know about people's characters and what they did – and you're always thinking "What would the captain think about this?"' Ingleby reveals that his grandfather was on HMS *Belfast* in the British Navy during World War

Two, and told him that it was just the same: that 'it never stops. You sleep, you work, you sleep. That's it. These men worked *really* hard.'

'But in relation to the life of the seamen,' says **Ed Woodall** of the officer-class, 'our life was pretty stylish.' As **Second Lieutenant Mowett** (and naval poet) 'I have a servant, if not two. I've got someone to put my boots on, someone to put my coat on, someone to shine my sword. I have a cabin to sleep in – well it's actually a little box. Not that we see a lot of that in the movie,' he adds, 'but that's the background of it. And officers have money to buy their own food, so we do manage to live rather well. There will always', he adds with a grin, 'be enough wine to see us through.'

Naval officers who fancied themselves as poets weren't uncommon (O'Brian borrowed most of Mowett's poetry from one William Falconer, a Scottish poet and merchant seaman). Woodall says that was one of the attractions of the part: 'to play on the one hand an expert seaman and a great fighter but also someone who, at night, settles down, gets his candle and his quill out and writes poems. Mowett's poems aren't about things like love; they're all about rigging and storms. And hulls... the man's obsessed by whatever ship he's on.' It sounds amusing to

*'Mowett's a poet, you know,' says Ed Woodall of his character. 'He's a sensitive man. But when it comes to the final battle, this guy is a butcher...'*

*Billy Boyd as coxswain Barrett Bonden. 'We wanted to get across the idea that this character has injuries from boxing, like he has in the books. So he's got scars from bare-knuckle boxing – from a scar on his cheekbone right down to scar tissue on his knuckles.'*

us: indeed, much of it is meant to be amusing to the crew, but Woodall acknowledges the serious undertones. 'He doesn't understand things on land, you know. Land to him... to a lot of the men... is a completely alien place. The sea is where you want to be. It's as if when you get on land you wobble – physically and psychologically.'

Alliteration accompanies **Billy Boyd** on set: he plays coxswain **Barrett Bonden**. 'Bonden's been with Captain Aubrey basically all his life. Really, he's been at sea all his life – and when they go on shore he's Aubrey's servant. So he's always with him. Jack Aubrey is his mentor.' Playing a character who was literally born at sea, Boyd imbibed all the research – including the grog. 'You know, these guys were drunk a lot of the time. They had their ration of grog – rum and water – every day.' Then, laughing, Boyd recalls a night prior to filming. 'Peter had made some grog to the actual recipe of the time, so we all sat around having dinner, getting slowly drunk on grog. Just to see what it was like. I wonder if that explains some of the courage from these battles?

*Max Pirkis as Lord Blakeney. At 13, the youngest midshipman on board – and a juvenile war-wounded. He loses his right arm in the first encounter with the* Acheron.

Yet some of these sailors weren't even fully grown. Playing larger roles than their characters do in any of O'Brian's books are **Max Pirkis (Lord Blakeney)** and **Max Benitz (Calamy)**.

*Midshipman Calamy (right), played by Max Benitz. Jack posthumously promotes him to the rank of acting Third Lieutenant, ensuring a pension for his mother.*

Both midshipmen, they illustrate the curious role of 'officers in training' of the era: some of them are children – Blakeney is thirteen – yet they're treated like adults, with attendant responsibilities. Jack Aubrey likes young people and, as regards Calamy, Max Benitz says that 'part of the back story is that my father has died, so there's a sort of father-son thing going on between Calamy and Aubrey.' Initially a minor part, the role of Calamy grew and he became 'quite a little hero. You know, he goes out on that raft (a decoy for the *Acheron*) and I like to think that's my first command…' At the age of seventeen, Calamy is something of an old hand 'and so I take Blakeney under my wing and look after him. There's a kind of family thing on a ship like this, you know…'

Blakeney's father is Will Garren, a friend of Jack's. 'So,' says Max Pirkis, 'when I come on board he makes sure things go well. And when I have my arm amputated, he really looks after me.' Having one arm was 'really weird. I have a body suit in my costume, which fattens one side of my body (the left side). And I have to put my right arm down my trousers. It was a bit of a pain: I'm right-handed and I presume my character is as well. So having to do stuff left-handed – swords, pistols, writing, even eating – was virtually impossible at first. I cheated a bit in boot camp,' he confides cheerfully.

Someone who cheated even more – as a character – was assistant surgeon **Higgins**, played by **Richard McCabe**. He's primarily employed as a tooth-puller (Maturin, famously, hates pulling teeth), effecting extractions with his bare hands. But, says McCabe, 'he's not a sailor. And he's not at all competent as a surgeon either. He's absolutely terrified by the whole thing – and there's a lot of scope for

*ABOVE Higgins, played by Richard McCabe. Employed by Stephen as Assistant Surgeon, he knows next nothing about surgery. And he's highly inventive about pulling teeth...*

*RIGHT Ship's carpenter Mr Lamb (Tony Dolan). Note the woolly 'thrum cap'. Apparently all ships' carpenters wore this distinctive headgear in order to be easily spotted when there was a lot of activity on board. This is the first outing for a thrum cap in the history of film ...*

humour in that.' In O'Brian's *The Far Side of the World*, Higgins suffers an ignominious fate – being tossed overboard after botching an abortion on Mrs Hollar, the only female on board. The only female on board in the film, however, was Aspasia the goat. 'If she could talk,' jokes McCabe, 'what a tale she would tell...' And then, more seriously, 'She actually became enormously popular. It's great to have an animal on board, It makes you realise that, whilst they had livestock to kill and eat, some animals were pets. They even took birds on board – and Bonden has a dog, you know. They became enormously important, those animals; home comforts for when they were out at sea for great lengths of time.'

Higgins is one of the least whiskery characters on board: his portion of sideburns appears to have been given to ship's carpenter **Mr Lamb**, played by **Tony Dolan**. A warrant officer employed by the Navy, his role, as Dolan says, 'is to keep the King's ship in good condition through good and bad, through storms and battles and so on.' In this movie, he has his work cut out – and the additional burden of disguising the *Surprise* as a whaler. Effecting that ruse meant some major changes: 'The transom, for example, which is the back of this ship, is a particular shape. The French captain has seen our backside before so we have to change it. That's a lot of work. And we repaint the ship: we dress it as a whaler. I even have to build an oven for boiling

*Bryan Dick, as carpenter's mate Nagle, jokes that 'We turn up every day and get covered in filth. Basically, that's how the make-up works…'*

down whale oil. It's another challenge: we aren't just pretending to be a whaler – we have to *be* a whaler.'

**Bryan Dick**, playing carpenter's mate **Nagle**, was struck by a different sort of challenge. 'It must have been so *lonely* at sea. There's just nothing around you, and we were only a few miles out (when filming on the *Rose*). There was nothing around these guys for months on end. Nothing but sea. At night,' he adds, 'it's black. Complete, pitch blackness. It's spooky, but it's great.' Not so great was being flogged for insubordination, but 'I had a rubber back piece made for that sequence: it's a wool whip but I actually got caught by it a couple of times and it stings like hell. Imagine what it would have been like if it was a rope whip…' Then he adds that there was a pay-off: 'They shaded muscles into the back piece so that I look butch. Now isn't that good?'

But Nagle had to cut his friend Warley loose from the fallen rigging, consequently sending him to his death. 'It makes you think… they had to make those kind of decisions every day at sea. People died all the time – it really was a horrifically hard life.'

**Joe Morgan**, as **Warley**, spent 'two weeks in the tank drowning'. Prior to death, he was captain of the mizzen-top, and spent most of his time aloft. 'I think it's about a hundred and ten foot to the top of the mast. That was pretty scary at first. So was climbing over the rigging, which goes outwards, so you're actually leaning backwards as you climb.' Morgan recounts this in a breezy, matter-of-fact manner – belying the fact (which he didn't admit at the time – but then who would?) that he started off being scared of heights…

*Joe Morgan had to overcome a fear of heights to play Warley, captain of the mizzen mast. He was rewarded with a two-week stint drowning in the tank.*

*Patrick Gallagher as
Awkward Davies.
O'Brian described the
character as an
'unhandy brute'.*

*Like some other
actors, William
Mannering (Faster
Doudle) began
researching his role in
England, even going
to sailing school. At
that point, he wasn't
aware of what the
Baja boot camp
would have in store
for him…*

And in the movie, in a scene in the Great Cabin, it looks like Warley's scared of Jack. 'No, I'm just tongue-tied in front of authority. Although I'm in charge of my own little crew, I'm withdrawn in front of the captain. And I wouldn't normally be in the Great Cabin.' It's a reminder that the tiny wooden world of the *Surprise* was, whilst one unit, composed of rigid hierarchies with the captain at the top. And here's a good example of how they viewed the captain: 'They just place blind trust in him. You know, he's Lucky Jack, he'll get them through and they… well, they love him as a captain. They completely trust him.'

At the opposite end of the scale is **Awkward Davies**, a huge, violent and brutal seaman described in the books as verging on madness. **Patrick Gallagher** laughs and agrees that his character is really on board because he 'fights like a whirling dervish. Basically, he likes to kill people. A lot.' But there's another layer here: 'Jack actually saved Davies' life in another book, so that's why I sort of follow him around.'

'What I think makes this film unique,' continues Gallagher, 'is that it's not about Jack Aubrey, about Hollywood stars and epic battles. It's about us – eating, drinking, working on the ship. It's about the period and it tells a story: that's what sets it aside.

**Faster Doudle** (so named because he moves slowly) is, as **William Mannering** says, 'a topman of the foremast – that's at the pointy end of the ship, as we professionals call it.' He also reveals that to play the part he had to 'get over my extreme fear of heights. Climbing through the futtock shrouds to the fighting top (where you invert and go back on yourself) is very frightening and very unnatural.' Not for his character, though. 'Yeah: he's brilliant at working with ropes and lines. I went to a sailing school before I left England to learn about knots and things.' Little did he suspect, at that point, that the boot camp would help him get into role. And the make-up. 'It's crisp, nasty, thick stuff. It's not Vidal Sassoon – but it's how it should be. It's superb. These guys had bits of tar in their hair – any time there was a rainstorm they'd be out there washing their hair – any opportunity to get clean and wash off all that salt as well.'

'If anybody asks me who he is, I just say he's the oldest man on the ship,' says **George Innes** of **Joe Plaice**. 'That's his only claim to fame. Until he has his trepanning operation. People are rather in awe of him after that. The operation,' explains Innes, 'is basically boring a hole in the skull to relieve pressure. I've heard it on good authority that people get a kick out of it. God knows how…'

Plaice is a gentle, knowing seaman who's been around the world about a thousand times. 'I think that anybody who survived even a year on those ships had to be extremely tough. They range from young kids to people my age – I mean how old am I? Sixty or something? How the kids endured it I'll never know. I don't think we can really imagine what they must have gone through.'

Stephen Maturin's manservant **Padeen** lurks in the background – and indeed the foreground – but doesn't say a word. 'But it's a giant role,' laughs **John De Santis**, 'I'm six foot ten.' Padeen *can* actually speak – but only in Gaelic, so it's implicit that he speaks to Stephen. 'He was picked up by Stephen in a lunatic asylum just prior to this voyage,' says De Santis. 'Not that he's remotely insane; it's just that he speaks a strange language, he's also got a cleft palate and, after getting himself into some sort of trouble, it was easiest to treat him as insane.' Harsh indeed, but, on the *Surprise*, the great thing is that 'nobody judges him. They treat him like the gentle, benevolent soul he is.'

ABOVE *'I just say he's the oldest man on the ship,' says George Innes of Joe Plaice. 'That's his only claim to fame.' That, and the dubious pleasure of being trepanned.*
BELOW *Maturin's gentle-giant manservant, played by John De Santis.*

*Chris Larkin as Captain Howard of the Marines. An integral part of the Royal Navy since 1664, the Marines were effectively ships' policemen; 'kind of the George Orwell people,' grins Larkin. But they were (and still are) required to fight as well – at land and when boarding enemy vessels.*

*Robert Pugh plays The Master Allen, second in command as regards sailing tactics and techniques. A tough job when Jack Aubrey, the first in command, has a habit of sailing pretty close to the wind...*

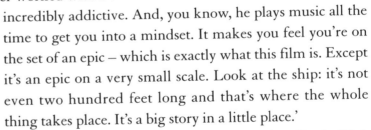

**Chris Larkin, Captain Howard** of the Marines, having come here straight from the set of a boat-bound drama, says that 'I think this is my destiny: to be stuck on boats, working on all-male films. That seems to be it,' he laughs. 'I would like to work with an actress. It would be really nice. But,' he adds, 'working with Peter is extraordinary. I've never worked with a director who has so much enthusiasm. It's incredibly addictive. And, you know, he plays music all the time to get you into a mindset. It makes you feel you're on the set of an epic – which is exactly what this film is. Except it's an epic on a very small scale. Look at the ship: it's not even two hundred feet long and that's where the whole thing takes place. It's a big story in a little place.'

'I'm playing **The Master Allen,**' says **Robert Pugh**. 'He's second in command regarding the sailing tactics and techniques.' He adds that he's 'rather upset by the tactics of the captain, but secretly I think I greatly admire him. He's unorthodox in how he sails the boat and how he gets involved in various skirmishes with the enemy. Like Nelson, he doesn't play it by the book. There are certain rules and protocol you must stick with in battle, but Aubrey doesn't do that. He's not from the school I'm from – it's like he's the new kid on the block as regards tactics. But at the end of the day you judge by results – and that's usually success with Aubrey.'

*Ian Mercer as Hollar the bosun (officially spelled, but not pronounced 'boatswain'). He manages all the rigging work on board – and that means everything to do with the twenty-five miles of rope and more than twenty sails.*

**Ian Mercer** says playing **Hollar** the bosun means that 'you don't really get involved in any popularity contests: the day-to-day rule of the ship is your domain so everybody's going to hate you at some point during the day. Every line and sheet has to be kept in order, every piece of canvas has to be accounted for, and the day-to-day discipline is in his charge as well.' When there's plenty of action going on, whether it be in battle or during a storm, discipline isn't a problem. But on a bad day – in the doldrums – 'two hundred men with nothing to do means two hundred problems'.

'There is,' continues Mercer, 'a lot of ad-libbing with Peter, he likes to film things that just turn up, which means I have a lot of ordering around to do in the background. And that's where our advisors prove invaluable: they can keep me right if I'm issuing unexpected orders.' Advisors dressed as extras, that is, lurking in the background…

*Mark Lewis Jones as Hogg the whaling captain, a character who, in the O'Brian book, is more than a little stunned by naval hierarchy and discipline.*

In O'Brian's *The Far Side of the World*, **Hogg the Whaler** is shocked by the rigours of Naval discipline. He is played in the movie by **Mark Lewis Jones**, who muses 'Maybe that's why they're better sailors than whalers…' The whalers arrived on set later than the crew of the *Surprise*, 'but we had our own little boot camp. Lots of rowing, like we're doing when the *Surprise* comes to

*Alex Palmer as Slade.
'It's always exciting
for an actor,' he says
of the boot camp,
'to be trained to do
something different.
We're never, ever,
going to fire cannons,
but we do get a taste
of what it might have
been like.'*

*Jack Randall and
Richard Pates as,
respectively,
Midshipmen Boyle
and Williamson. Of
their youth, Richard
Pates remarks that 'I
think that's one of the
points of this film…
there were children
who had to do some
quite hectic things: go
into battle, actually
kill people.'*

the rescue. I'd like to think we add another impetus to the story. Our costumes certainly do: I've got these enormous boots and this huge, long wig. They do the acting for you…'

**Alex Palmer**, seaman **Slade**, elaborates on the practice of tattooing. 'Slade does most of the tattoos, using a pin and ink, and it could be pretty dangerous. The "grand masters" would have used a chisel-type thing, but Slade just uses this very sharp spike. You could get blood poisoning if the pin went in too far. And I can vouch for how painful a home-made one is: I've got one I did when I was fifteen.'

Coincidentally, fifteen was the average age of a midshipman in 1805. Midshipmen **Williamson** and **Boyle**, played by **Richard Pates** and **Jack Randall**, spent 'a lot of time playing pranks with each other,' according to Pates, 'which is exactly what midshipmen did a lot of the time in the books. At first I thought Williamson would just be a prankster, but I've been given a few scenes where you see him collapsing and quaking with fear. And you can see him doing a couple of relay jobs – passing messages to the captain. He's developing and learning.' Boyle, however, is 'less intellectual than the others,' says Jack Randall. 'He hasn't a clue what he's doing when it comes to charts and so on. And it must have been awkward, you know, bossing around men who were twenty or thirty years older than you.'

But that's what life was like at sea: a life that this movie strives to portray in all its variations.

## *Casting the Net Far and Wide*

One of the many unusual aspects of this film is the sheer number of actors and extras required, on a permanent basis, on set. Twenty-five principal actors spent five months in Baja: so did a core group of fifty-five extras, joined, at different junctures, by up to two hundred more. Peter Weir admits, 'I've never had that before.' It's more common for actors to fly in and out to a set as required, and for extras to be occasional adjuncts to the main picture. Not here. Not on a set that, from the very beginning, was designed to operate exactly like a ship's company.

The principal actors were cast by Mary Selway in London, who has a string of credits as diverse as *Indiana Jones and the Temple of Doom*, *Emma* and *Notting Hill* to her name. She also has a BAFTA Award for Outstanding Contribution to British Film.

The extras, however, came from all over the world, echoing the reality of a British crew (most crews, for that matter) of two centuries ago. In O'Brian's novels, Jack often points out that a huge proportion of those hauling the ropes weren't 'hearts of oak' at all but were Bengalis, Finns, Italians, Poles and Greeks.

When Peter Weir came to think about casting the extras, he reflected on a more recent past – the destruction of the Berlin Wall and the collapse of Communism. 'Suddenly we were getting television images from the old Soviet

*Extras were cast from as far afield as Poland, Canada and Sudan.*

bloc – and I'll never forget looking at those faces. They were quite different, you know. I remember thinking "Oh, they haven't eaten our food; they might be my age but they haven't eaten the same food. They've not been to the movies. They've not had the stimulation. They've not had those 'Kodak' moments; no concept of an image to project to the screen…" so I just filed it away in the back of my mind – and when it came to this film I remembered it. I recalled it.'

He also recalled (in the sense of recommissioning) someone he had worked with before; Judy Bouley, who became the Additional Casting Director on this movie. Initially, he wanted her to find a crew entirely from Poland, but budgetary concerns restricted them to eleven. These extras were cast by Marek Zydowicz and Kazimierz Suwala – extras who, in the director's words, became 'the fore-ground of the background. I didn't think Judy could get me the equivalent faces in America,' he continues. She could – and she did. 'We have,' says Bouley, 'eleven people from Poland; we have a Canadian Greek [O'Brian's 'Old Sponge'] and we have people from Sudan, Senegal, Mexico and the States.'

They range in age from ten to fifty-five, and most of them had never seen a movie camera before, let alone appeared in front of one. Bouley and her associate Tom Gustavsen travelled for four months to find her extras, met over 7000 people and interviewed 450. Of that number, Peter Weir chose the final fifty-five. All of them were trained at the actors' boot camp on this film. All of them were here for the entire five-month duration of the shoot. Only some of them have character names in the script. Very few of them deliver any lines. Most of them will be seen only fleetingly.

The question that springs to mind is 'Why?' Why go to so much trouble to select people who are, basically, part of the scenery? That's just the point. Everything in this film, background and foreground, is about creating a three-dimensional picture; a world at sea that reflected, two hundred years ago, an entire community of, as mentioned above, wildly differing nationalities. 'Peter said to me,' recalls Bouley, 'that he wanted me to find men who were not modern men: men from another time. Guileless men: the best of men and the worst of men. And that we should love them for their faults.' Bouley pauses and points out that this is her forty-second movie (previous films include *Evita, Castaway, Fearless* and *The Perfect Storm*) and then adds, with conviction, 'And you know what? I can quit now. It doesn't get any better than this.'

Looking at the faces, meeting the people she has cast, one can see her point. These people look as if they're from another age, place and culture. And, to varying degrees, they look haunted. And they all look markedly different from each other. Peter Weir – again this is unusual – knew them all by name and, crucially, by individual look, 'so sometimes I'd say: "Get me Pavel. Put him on the left there with the

majority of the Polish crew and put Jakob there with Russell" – another Russell – and, you know, I'd put it together like a painting where I'd have thirty or forty faces and, you know, with the lighting it wouldn't be far off a painting of that era – and that's because of the faces, clothing and the setting. But above all the faces.'

Staggeringly diverse in look, the extras also came from wildly different backgrounds. An apple farmer from California, an engineering graduate from Krakow in Poland, a street-sweeper from Tijuana and a Sudanese refugee have pretty well nothing in common. Again, that's the point.

Take this extract from *The Wooden World*, historian N.A.M. Rodger's seminal study of the Georgian Navy, and one sees fact conjoining with film. 'There were men from every nation under heaven in the Navy, sometimes swept up in the press (The Impressment Service), but more often volunteers. Cretans, Danes, Italians, Portugese, Swedes, Hanoverians, Americans of every colony and every colour, they appear in almost all ships' musters.' Rodger is fascinating on the subject of colour, later detailing a court martial ending with the sentencing of two white men to death, largely on the evidence of the principal prosecution witness – a black seaman: 'an interesting illustration of the Navy's relatively liberal outlook on questions of colour.'

*Guileless, haunted and, above all, 'from another era' were the prerequisites for the 'look' of the background sailors on the* Surprise.

*Benjamin Akuetoc (left), originally from Sudan. Echoing the reality of two hundred years ago, seamen in the movie were from every race, creed and colour.*

The Navy's attitude to race and colour, says the author, 'was liberal by the standards of the societies from which they had come, and it is easy to see the attractions of a world in which a man's professional skill mattered more than his colour.'

Judy Bouley, too, was interested in professional skills. The ship she was manning could well have been at sea for two years; carrying enough supplies and craftsmen to practically rebuild herself if the need arose. So she needed not just sailors and marines but carpenters, blacksmiths, musicians… again, a whole community. She needed to mirror, on screen, what Patrick O'Brian had on paper. And she reached out by distributing flyers in sailing clubs and tall ship societies, posting advertisements on websites and radio stations; she went into boats, bars, dockyards and backstreets and to out-of-the-way towns.

A member of the Santa Cruz sailing club, who heard in the clubhouse about Bouley and her quest, thought he'd try 'on a whim' because he had no plans for the summer. He remembers being completely pole-axed when Bouley suddenly 'got this really stern look on her face and said, "Okay, it's 1805, you're twenty-two years old and you're standing before the captain and the officers on a ship. What do you say? What does your background say about you? What do you do? Do you believe in God?"'. He had to quickly invent a background, including even background interests. He was aided in the latter by the fact that 'I had my jaw-harp with me. I am,' he adds defensively, 'originally from Arkansas'.

Benjamin Akuetoc is originally from Sudan and didn't have to invent a harrowing background. Aged five, he lost his family to war and fled through jungles and rivers across the border to Ethiopia. By the age of fourteen he was in the military and engaged in armed combat. Eventually, in Kenya, he was assisted to the United States. By some curious twist of fate he arrived in America on 11 September 2001. And when Judy Bouley came to audition him – after asking at the Alliance for African Assistance – he was working as a bagger in a grocery store in San Diego. 'I'm happy here,' he says on location. 'I like having everybody with me. I don't like to sit alone thinking too much, because it takes me back to Africa…'

Gerard Powell, a real-life extra from Hollywood, has never seen an ensemble like this. He admits that when he first saw the motley crew of different nationalities, he feared they'd never get through five months without some unscripted fights. The opposite happened: they bonded to form a community. 'And you know,' Powell says, 'if we'd all been extras from Hollywood, this just would not have worked.'

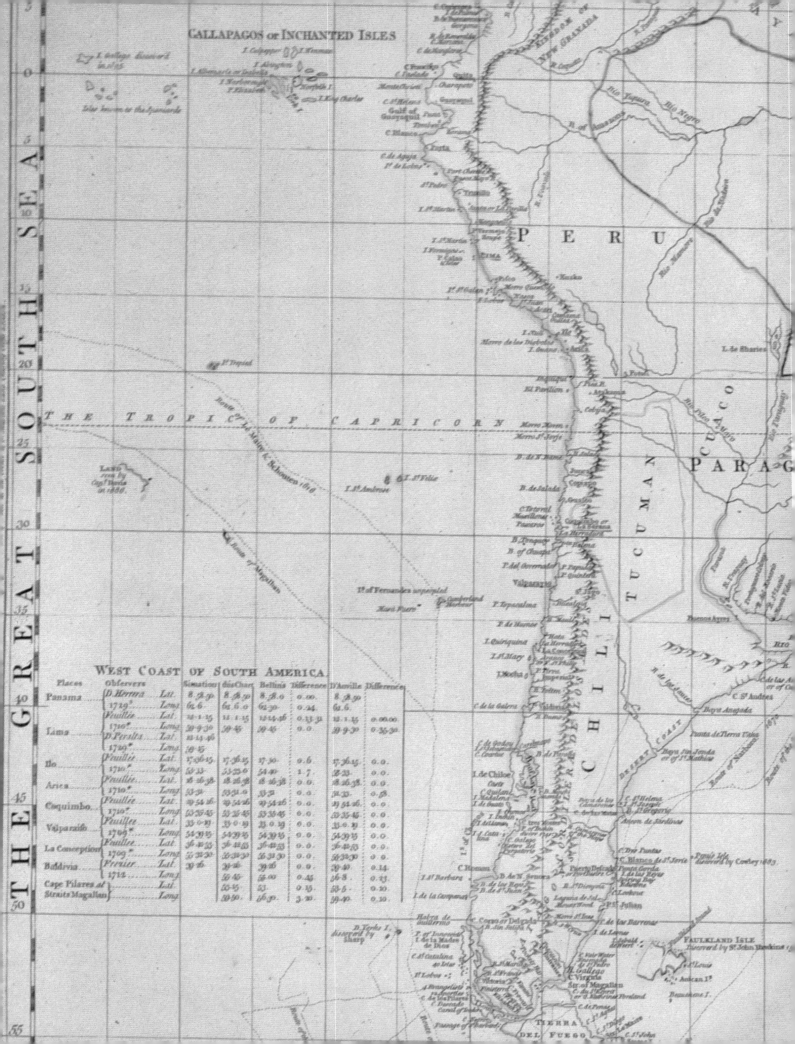

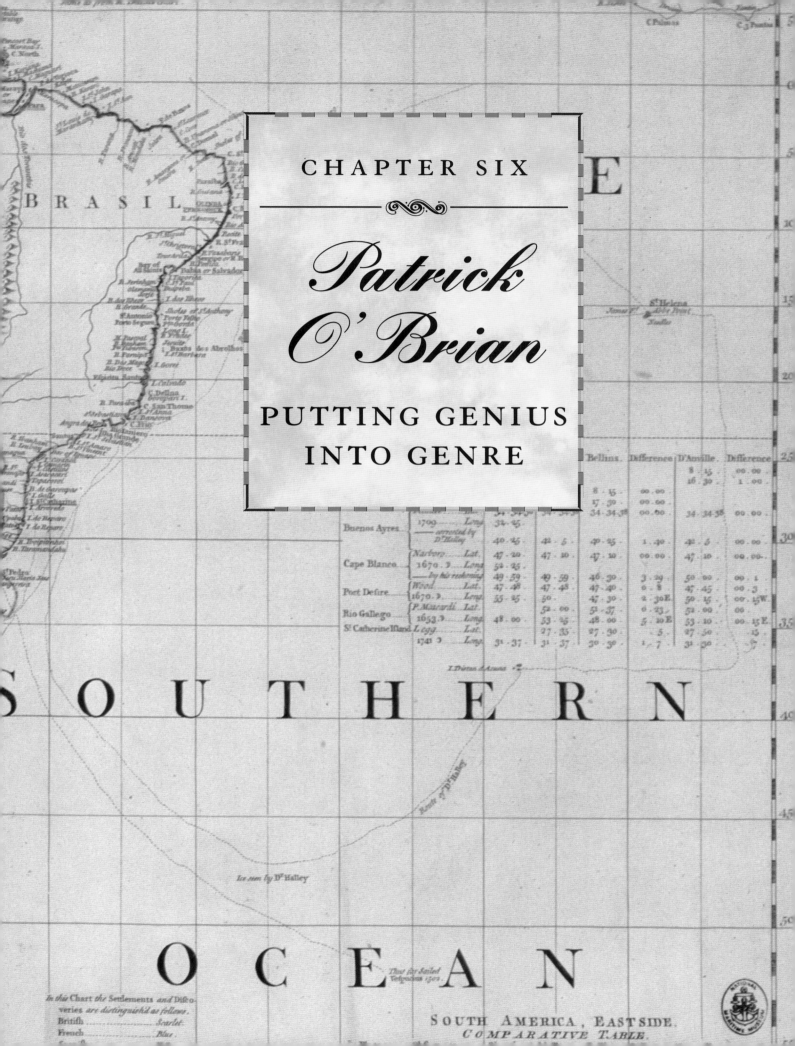

# CHAPTER SIX

## Patrick O'Brian

### PUTTING GENIUS INTO GENRE

Best known for his twenty Aubrey/Maturin tales, Patrick O'Brian is the author of several other novels and short stories as well as the highly acclaimed biographer of Picasso, and of the naturalist and politician Sir Joseph Banks. He also translated many works from French to English, among them the novels and memoirs of Simone de Beauvoir and the first volume of Jean Lacouture's biography of Charles de Gaulle. In 1995 he was awarded the CBE (Commander of the British Empire) and, in 1997, he was given an honorary doctorate of letters by Trinity College, Dublin.

Born near London in 1914, he died in Dublin in January 2000. For most of his adult life (since 1949) he lived in Collioure near Perpignan in southern France with his wife Mary, who died in 1998. For much of that time, he lived in relative poverty and obscurity. The first of the Aubrey/Maturin novels, published in 1970, was to mark a sea change in his fortunes…

'I am often asked,' he wrote, 'how I came to write about the sea. It happened like this: in the early fifties, when I had finished a couple of difficult novels, one of them quite good but filled with anguish and written with even more, it occurred to me to write a book for fun.'

The first of those 'difficult' books, *Testimonies*, was rapturously reviewed by the critic Delmore Schwartz in 1953. He rated it superior to Hemingway's *The Old Man and the Sea*, Steinbeck's *East of Eden* and Waugh's *Men at Arms*. Yet, to the wider American public, O'Brian remained unknown for almost forty years.

That book O'Brian wrote for 'fun', based on the factual voyage of Captain Anson in 1740, was called *The Golden Ocean* and was met, according to its author, with 'frigid indifference' by critics and the public alike.

O'Brian goes on to relate how another publisher suggested he try his hand at the sea again and that 'I was perfectly happy to do so. I knew the element tolerably well, having sailed in most rigs, and naval history had been my delight ever since I bought the six volumes of Beatson before the war and those of James a little later.'

The book was set in the middle of the Napoleonic Wars, a prolonged conflict referred to by O'Brian as 'the later English-speaking people's Troy Tale, as capable

PREVIOUS SPREAD
*A contemporary map showing the journey undertaken in* The Far Side of the World.

*Patrick O'Brian at a dinner in his honour in the Painted Hall at Greenwich. One of the greatest tributes made to a living author, the guest list included the American Ambassador, the former British Ambassador to Washington, eight British and two American admirals.*

of infinite variation and extension as the countless successors to *The Iliad*'. It was called *Master & Commander* and was published in 1970. 'Once again,' O'Brian recalled, 'the public turned a deaf ear, a blind eye.'

Yet his publishers did not. Although the book was commissioned in the United States, it was first published in the UK, where, with its successors in what was to become the Aubrey/Maturin series, it gained respect and increasing momentum.

The publishing history in the US was less satisfactory: five books were published under various imprints before grinding to a halt. Then Norton & Co started republishing the series in 1990 – to immediate acclaim. 'The best novelist you've never heard of' (*New York Times*) quickly became an international bestseller and the intensely private Patrick O'Brian, likened to Austen, Dickens, Melville and Conrad, was catapulted into the headlines. Everyone wanted to know more about him.

But O'Brian abhorred conversation about himself, and had an absolute loathing of personal questions, even if they were posed by friends. He was adamant that his books, not his life, were the only legitimate objects of curiosity about him and that posterity should concern itself with the works and not the man. In many ways that is a shame because, as his American editor Starling Lawrence says, 'He was simply one of the most interesting and complex people I've ever met – and one of the funniest. He was *very* amusing'. Arabella Pike, his British counterpart, adds that 'I adored him. He was fascinating and tremendously good company... extraordinarily courteous, yet he was also a brilliant tease.' She goes on to mention his 'twinkle' could turn into 'a reptilian glare' if his personal life was being intruded upon by others. 'He thought personal questions were the *height* of rudeness.'

So did Stephen Maturin. In the novel *Clarissa Oakes (The True Love)*, we're told that he didn't regard question and answer as a civilised form of conversation; and thought it 'extremely ill-bred'. And in *Master & Commander* we learn something that is reiterated throughout the series: Stephen was 'a naturally secretive man'; that 'the power of keeping his mouth shut was innate.' Maturin, in many ways, *was* Patrick O'Brian.

O'Brian freely acknowledged that he and Maturin shared passions (particularly natural history – O'Brian said he 'couldn't remember not having an interest in birds') and that, like Maturin, he had worked in intelligence. Although he refuted suggestions of self-identification through this most complex of characters, he also shared Maturin's fluency in French, Spanish and Catalan, although not his facility with the cello: O'Brian was highly knowledgeable about music but did not play any instrument. The two were even similar in appearance. And Maturin was half-Irish whilst O'Brian, curiously, claimed to be wholly Irish. That was, in fact,

wholly untrue. He was of German descent, his grandfather having emigrated from Leipzig to London in the 1860s.

It's now well known that O'Brian's punctilious attention to historical accuracy didn't extend to his own early life. He remained silent about the fact that, in 1945, he had changed his name from Richard Patrick Russ and that when he married that same year it was for the second time. If those, combined with inconsistencies about his childhood years, were the reasons for his extreme aversion to personal questions, his greatest disservice seemed to have been to himself. As Starling Lawrence says, 'I really don't care who he was or who he wasn't except that it seemed to be a problem for him.'

Personal friends also knew not to ask about his background nor to steer discussions towards the intimate. One of them, the actor Charlton Heston, remarked in a documentary that 'he is a visitor from the early nineteenth century – although I wouldn't dream of discussing that with him.'

The first part of that statement is by far the more fascinating. One of the most interesting thing about Patrick O'Brian – and probably the reason why he's credited with putting genius into the genre of the historical novel – was that he really seemed to prefer to inhabit the early nineteenth century and not the late twentieth century. The degree of erudition in the Aubrey/Maturin series and O'Brian's absolute mastery of an entire world suggests someone writing *in* an era and not *of* it. He moves, for example, with remarkable ease from the comparative anatomy of an orang-utan to abstruse naval terms without losing a lightness of touch… 'It's the detail and the wit that are so extraordinary,' says Starling Lawrence. 'You could read each book several times before you picked up all the sly references: there's a *huge* amount of learning behind these books. You really have to know what you're talking about to have a character get something humorously wrong,' he finishes, with reference to Jack and Stephen's squabbles about subjects ranging from the finer points of navigation to the elder Bach.

But for all O'Brian's nineteenth-century sensibilities, for all that he seemed to pride himself on living 'very much out of this world', he didn't seem entirely unhappy in it. Those who knew him well agreed that his rigidly formal manner

*No one who knew O'Brian missed the similarities between the author and Stephen Maturin. They shared a passion for natural history, an interest in music and they even looked similar. The austere twinkle could, in both men, turn into a reptilian glare as the shutters went down on personal questions.*

and almost precious politeness hid a much freer character. And part of him relished the brouhaha surrounding him in later life.

Richard Ollard, his British editor from 1967–1987, responding to a question about his famously private author, acknowledged with a wry smile that secrecy 'wasn't uncongenial to him'. Stuart Proffitt, who succeeded Ollard, says somewhat elliptically that 'little by little, he started talking'. Arabella Pike, who was his last editor, says that by the late 1990s he was comfortable with some aspects of his fame. He evidently enjoyed the respect he accorded: how could anyone not enjoy what, in 1996, was one of the greatest ever tributes paid to a living author? William Waldegrave, then the Chief Secretary to the Treasury, hosted a dinner in the Painted Hall at Greenwich Naval College in O'Brian's honour. The guest list included eight British admirals, two American admirals, the American Ambassador, the Chairman of the Governors of the BBC, the Minister of the Armed Forces, the Head of the British Intelligence Services MI5 and MI6 (allegedly) and the entire complement of the Cayman Islands Branch of the Patrick O'Brian Appreciation Society…

It was success on the other side of an ocean that O'Brian had crossed so famously in fiction that he really enjoyed; it seems to have brought out the Jack Aubrey in him. 'You would have thought,' says Starling Lawrence, 'that he was a prime candidate to be repulsed by America. He made three long publicity trips over here and I went absolutely everywhere with him because, frankly, I thought the unadulterated dose of American culture would kill him.'

*Patrick O'Brian at a dinner given in his honour. Beneath the rigidly formal exterior lay a much freer, and highly amusing, character. By the late 1990s he had become comfortable with – even to actively relish – aspects of his fame.*

O'Brian, it transpires, *was* shocked by the presumption of people who came up to him, called him by his first name and asked him where he was born, yet he developed an 'undisguised but very complicated affection for the United States and the kind of reception he got here. People came to, if you like, "touch the hem of the garment" – to worship – and that sort of thing just doesn't happen in England.' Lawrence recalls a man at a book signing in Washington who had driven all the way from Iowa ('I repeat – Iowa. Get a map and look. You can't even drive that far in England…') to obtain O'Brian's signature on a couple of books. 'O'Brian loved it. He said something to the effect that the only thing he required of his public was unstinting and unmeasured praise. And he got it…'

O'Brian himself, writing about a publicity tour of the east coast, was predictably more reticent, but unfailingly polite. 'It was wearing but infinitely rewarding – until one has eaten cod and clam chowder in Boston, one has not fully lived. And the television there was surprisingly discreet.' The mention of food is characteristic of O'Brian; anyone who reads the books cannot doubt his passion for good food and fine wine.

But what would O'Brian have made of the movie? Starling Lawrence reckons that he 'would have a reflexive disdain for the enterprise that mirrored his attitude to the book's success here: more apparent than real. He would have complained and pretended it wasn't very important to him, but clearly it would have been, I think he would have enjoyed the hoopla over the movie.'

No one will ever know, but O'Brian's editor certainly doesn't evince any disdain of his own. 'I think it's wonderful it's gone to this step. I know they have taken astonishing care, and he deserves that. I was terrified this was going to be some sloppy, stupid thing, and that certainly hasn't happened. I can't think of anyone whose reputation deserves this more.'

# Reviews

'To read a first novel by an unknown author which, sentence by sentence and page by page, makes one say: he can't keep going at this pitch, the intensity is bound to break down, the perfection of tone can't be sustained – is to rejoice in an experience of pleasure and astonishment.'                    DELMORE SCHWARTZ, 1953

This review was for O'Brian's novel *Testimonies*, which he referred to as one of his 'difficult' books. The book is set in Wales, and predated the Aubrey/Maturin series by sixteen years, but some sort of seed was sewn: the names Aubrey and Maturin both appear in the book.

The review was something of a lone voice at the time, and not until O'Brian was in his seventies did his naval 'tales' receive worldwide recognition as true, literary masterpieces upon which praise has been consistently lavished.

'The action scenes, battles, chases, storms, shipwrecks are brilliantly described in vivid and impeccable prose. The romantic passages, the erudite descriptions of flora and fauna throughout the world, the humour and general atmosphere of enlightened civilisation are all remarkable. But, above all, it is the characters who make these stories unique… This saga, which, I ardently hope, is still a long way from its end, already adds up to one of the greatest achievements of contemporary fiction.'
*Sunday Telegraph*

'The pleasures of Patrick O'Brian's Aubrey/Maturin novels defy enumeration… these are books that offer the reader both sensual and intellectual enjoyment, the pleasures of immensely stylish writing as well as the pleasures of engagement with an author who is moralist, naturalist, and naval historian into the bargain… Meticulously researched and heart-stoppingly vivid… Few books boast the richly imagined central figures of these tales, or place them in such deeply researched settings.'

*Washington Post Book World*

'Taken together, the novels are a brilliant achievement. They display staggering erudition on almost all aspects of early nineteenth-century life, with impeccable period detail… [Compared to Forester's characters] Aubrey and Maturin are subtler, richer items; in addition Patrick O'Brian has a gift for the comic which Forester lacks.'

*Times Literary Supplement*

'Patrick O'Brian presents the lost arcana of that hard-pressed, cruel, courageous world with an immediacy that makes its workings both comprehensible and fascinating. But in the end it is the serious exploration of human character that gives the books their greatest power: the fretful play of mood that can irrationally darken the edges of the brightest triumph, and that can feed a trickle of merriment into the midst of terror and tragedy.'

*New York Times Book Review*

'O'Brian's books are as atypical of conventional sea stories as Conrad's. Like John LeCarré, he has erased the boundary separating a debased genre from 'serious' fiction. O'Brian is a novelist, pure and simple, one of the best we have.'

*Los Angeles Times Book Review*

'Some of you… have never read a Patrick O'Brian novel. I beseech you to start now. Start with *Master & Commander*, which should be available in paperback from your nearest bookseller. And if he – or she – does not have a copy, then beat the wretched fellow.'

*Irish Times*

# THE WORKS OF PATRICK O'BRIAN

**Aubrey/Maturin novels
(in order of publication):**
*Master & Commander*
*Post Captain*
HMS *Surprise*
*The Mauritius Command*
*Desolation Island*
*The Fortune of War*
*The Surgeon's Mate*
*The Ionian Mission*
*Treason's Harbour*
*The Far Side of the World*
*The Reverse of the Medal*
*The Letter of Marque*
*The Thirteen-gun Salute*
*The Nutmeg of Consolation*
*Clarissa Oakes (The True Love)*
*The Commodore*
*The Wine-Dark Sea*
*The Yellow Admiral*
*The Hundred Days*
*Blue at the Mizzen*

**Other Novels**
*Caesar*
*Hussein*
*Testimonies*
*The Catalans*
*The Golden Ocean*
*The Unknown Shore*
*Richard Temple*

**Biographies**
*Picasso*
*Joseph Banks*

**Anthologies**
*A Book of Voyages*
*Collected Short Stories*

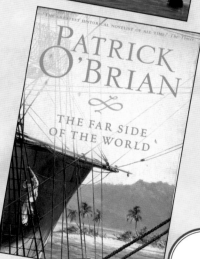

# GLOSSARY

**Articles of war:** regulations governing the conduct of men in the Royal Navy.

**Beat to quarters:** a drumroll to call all hands to 'battle stations'.

**Beating to weather:** sailing a zig-zag path into the weather to work upwind.

**Belaying pin:** carved wooden rods set in rails as points to secure lines.

**Bells:** the system of ringing of the ship's bell to mark time.

**Bending on:** rigging a sail into place so that it can be used.

**Block:** a pulley used in the rigging aboard a vessel.

**Boatswain, bosun, pronounced 'bo-sun':** manages all rigging work aboard.

**Broadside:** firing the guns on one side; or to be sideways to something.

**Butcher's bill:** phrase describing the list of casualties after a battle.

**Capstan:** the vertical winch used to haul heavy loads like the anchor.

**Carronade:** a powerful, short-barrelled deck gun used for short range.

**Cat's-paw:** a twisted loop in a line; or sea ripples in a breeze.

**Chains, chain plates:** fittings on the side of the hull which anchor the ship's rig.

**Chip log:** a wooden chip trailed off the stern to measure speed.

**Corble:** a sort of brace/bracket which protrudes from a wall to hold or support a weight above.

**Course:** the direction the ship is steered; also the lowest squaresail.

**Dead-eye and lanyard:** special permanent blocks and lines tensioning the standing rig.

**Defaulter:** one who has transgressed the ship's rules.

**Doldrums:** vast areas of steady, unchanging calm, usually near the tropics.

**Dowse, take, take-in:** remove the presence of a sail which is currently set.

**Ensign:** the flag flown aft which declares a ship's national identity.

**Fathom:** six feet, used for water depths or line lengths.

**Forecastle, foc's'l, pronounced 'fok-sul':** the ship's forward area, and its compartment.

**Foremast, fore:** a ship's forward-most mast. The lowest section, or its entirety.

**Frigate:** three-masted, full-rigged sailing ship with a single gundeck.

**Glass:** the on-deck hourglass; a telescope; or a barometer.

**Grating:** cross-slatted hatch covers, used upright to hold a man for flogging.

**Great cabin:** the captain's area aft, used as office and quarters.

**Halyard:** a line used to raise a sail when setting it.

**Hammock netting:** a mesh bin on deck to stow hammocks, providing protection in battle.

**Hawsers, warps:** heavy lines used for docking, towing, or mooring.

**Holy-stoning:** the scrubbing of decks using blocks of stone with sand and water.

**Jonah:** a person thought to bring bad luck to a ship.

**Larboard:** the left side of a vessel, now referred to as 'port'.

**Lay, laid:** the twist of rope strands, right (hawser-laid) or left (cable-laid).

**Leeward, pronounced 'loo-werd':** the side away from the wind, opposite windward.

**Lieutenant:** sea officer ranking after captain, the 'mate' on merchant ships.

**Main, mainmast:** a ship's second mast, or its lowest section.

**Midshipman:** officers-in-training, on board for education.

**Mizzen:** a ship's third mast. The lowest section, or its entirety.

**Powder monkey:** boy used to bring supplies from the powder magazine to the guns.

**Press, impressment:** to compel men to join a ship's crew.

**Preventer backstay:** temporary reinforcements of masts in unusually straining conditions.

**Quarterdeck:** the aft, raised portion of the weatherdeck.

**Rating, rated:** the levels earned by seamen, much as officers are 'ranked'.

**Royal:** a light-wind squaresail flown above the topgallants.

**Sailing master:** responsible for the ship's sailing and navigation, and crew training.

**Shoal:** shallow water, or an individual underwater hump.

**Spars:** wooden 'poles' that hold and spread the rigging and sails.

**Splinters:** a greater hazard to lives in wooden ship battles than the cannonballs creating them.

**Squaresails, square-rigged:** sails rigged perpendicular (square) to the ship's centreline.

**Standing rigging:** the 'fixed' lines and fittings installed to keep the spars in place.

**Starboard:** the right side of a vessel when looking forward.

**Studding sails, stunsails:** sails set on either side of the regular squares.

**Surgeon:** a vessel's medical officer, often with less training than a physician.

**Topgallant, t'gallant, t'gans'l, pronounced 't-gans-el':** a squaresail set above the topsail.

**Topmen:** sailors assigned to work aloft handling sails.

**Tops, fighting tops:** platforms on the lower mast for men handling sails or firing weapons.

**Topsail:** pronounced 'top-sul', a squaresail on the topmast, the second off the deck.

**Weather deck:** the uppermost deck comprised of the foredeck, waist, and quarterdeck.

**Weather gauge:** to be upwind of another ship, which has many advantages when in battle.

**Weevil:** beetles infamous for burrowing into provisions, especially grains and biscuits.

**Yard:** a horizontal spar which crosses the masts used to rig and set squaresails.